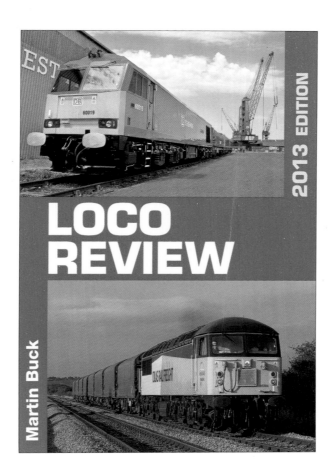

LOCO REVIEW

2013 EDITION

Martin Buck

FREIGHTMASTER

PUBLISHING

Contents

First published, November 2012 :

Freightmaster Publishing
158 Overbrook
SWINDON
SN3 6AY

www.freightmasterpublishing.co.uk

ISBN : 978-0-9558275-6-3

Printed :

Stephens & George
Goat Mill Road
Dowlais
MERTHYR TYDFIL
CF48 3TD
www.stephensandgeorge.co.uk

Cover Images :

No.60019 (top) at the port of Immingham. **Alan Padley**

No.56094 (bottom) at Ogden's Wood. **Richard Armstrong**

Opposite : Quite fitting in 'Diamond Jubilee' year, Deltic No.D9009 works 'The Elizabethan' charter on 25th July, which is seen passing Ryther (ECML). **Neil Harvey**

Note : All dates in the text are 2012, unless otherwise stated.

Setting the Scene

Welcome to *Loco Review - 2013*, which follows on from where the previous edition left off and with so much going on, some features have been be held over for the next edition, like celebrating 50-years of the Class 47s!

With only a limited number of pages to play with, coverage has to be selective and the aim of 'Loco Review' is to be a broad church of loco-hauled activity and not cover every weird and wonderful working that takes place, of which the latter is not feasible in any case!

It is hard to believe that a 'Deltic' should be hired in to work the Alcan 'trips' from North Blyth to Lynemouth in 2011, only for the flow to cease altogether a year later. That said, let's have a quick look at some of the positive things covered in Loco Review this time ....

- more Class 56s at work on the main line, thanks to Devon & Cornwall Railway making their 'grids' available for hire and Colas Rail resurrecting Nos.56087 and 56094, both looking great in Colas orange & black livery.

- DRS Class 57s find regular work on intermodal services between Tees Dock and Ditton.

- Harry Needle opts for orange as the colour for his fleet of Class 20s and GBRf adopt their own house colours for two of their 'on hire' Class 20s.

- GBRf celebrate 10 years in the intermodal market and brand No.66709 with an MSC container ship on the body side - smart!

- DBS are to be applauded for bringing more Class 60s out of store and back into main line action. The year starts with 11 'tugs' in traffic with a further 14 earmarked for overhaul, bringing the fleet number up to 25.

As for new freight flows, there are plenty, such as Teigngrace timber (Colas), Wentloog intermodal (DRS), Portbury biomass (GBRf), Dounreay flasks (DRS), Grangemouth fuel oil (Colas); not forgetting opencast blending coal from Earlseat to Hunterston - the first time freight has been seen on the Methil branch in Fife, Scotland, in more than 12 years.

On the heritage front, the iconic Class 52 'Westerns' and Class 73 'JAs' each celebrate a Golden Anniversary; we welcome back Class 50 No.50026 'Indomitable' and Class 26 No.26038 after more 20 years inactivity and I recall some special trains laid on to mark His Holiness the Pope's visit to the UK in May 1982.

I would like to thank to the photographers who have kindly contributed images for this book, especially those doing so for the first time - there really are some stunning images to show off. I try to accommodate everyone, but this is not always possible - please don't let this put you off if you missed out this time!

Finally, I must thank my wife, Joanne, for bearing long periods of preparation and research and, especially, proof-reading the script - it is appreciated!

Now, without further ado, please turn the page and enjoy the *2013 edition* at your leisure.

Martin Buck

GBRf - Ten Years After

Background

February 2002 sees GBRf venture into the freight sector with a contract from Mediterranean Shipping Company (MSC) to run intermodal trains out of the Port of Felixstowe, viz:

6E78, Felixstowe - Selby   6M73, Felixstowe - Hams Hall
6L79, Selby - Felixstowe   6L72, Hams Hall - Felixstowe

Traction is in the form of a GBRf Class 66/7 diesel loco.

Alan Padley

In fact, GBRf (Great Britain Railfreight), a subsidiary of GB Railway, entered into railfreight in March 2001 with 7 new Class 66/7 locos (Nos.66701 to 66707), painted in a striking 'bluebird' livery, based at Willesden. The '66/7' has a 92,000lbf tractive effort and a maximum speed of 75mph - initially, powering infrastructure trains in the east of England and East Anglia.

Since then, the GBRf fleet of Class 66/7s has grown to 46, plus 5 Class 92s as a result of the Company's tie up with Europorte in June 2010.

Intermodal Traffic (10th Anniversary)

GBRf's intermodal market has grown by over 400%, as you can see from the table on Page 6, with the initial four trains in 2002 increasing to 16 trains in February 2012. To celebrate the 10-year partnership with Mediterranean Shipping Company (MSC), GBRf name Class 66/7 No.66709 'Sorrento' on 25th April and the newly liveried loco is unveiled at a special ceremony at the Port of Felixstowe, where GBRf has its Intermodal headquarters (see Pages 14 and 15).

To mark this special anniversary, there now follows a pictorial record of GBRf intermodal services, both past and present.

4M23 : The unique liveried GBRf Class 66/7 No.66720 (above) passes through the relatively recently remodelled Rugby station with a well loaded 4M23, 10:45 Felixstowe North - Hams Hall intermodal. The delightful body side designs were the brainchild of six-year old Emily Goodman.   **Nathan Seddon**

Originally, 4E33 intermodal used to be routed over Great Eastern metals via Colchester before being re-routed via Ely - Peterborough - Nuneaton.

On 14th November 2007, original liveried No.66710 (right) passes Kelvedon (between Marks Tey and Witham) leading 4E33, the 11:00 Felixstowe South - Doncaster Railport.

At this time, GBRf was part of First Group and their corporate logo is clearly displayed on the front of the loco.

4E33

No.66714 'Cromer Lifeboat' (below) powers through Whittlesea on 24th February 2011 leading 4E33, 11:20 Felixstowe South - Doncaster Railport Intermodal. This service runs every week day and is a good time-keeper, pictured passing the camera on time.

The superbly maintained signal box at Whittlesea is of Great Eastern Railway design and dates from 1887.   **James Welham (2)**

4M29 : On 10th March, No.66718 'Gwyneth Dunwoody' (above) approaches Ketton crossing on 10th March with 4M29, 04:12 Felixstowe - Barton Dock intermodal. This train was originally launched under the 'interhub' banner in March 2011, running as 4M33, 23:20 Ripple Lane - Trafford Park.

GBRf Intermodal Departures (Weekdays) - February 2012

Barton Dock

Time	Code	Train	Traction	Notes	
11:28	4L18	Barton Dock - Felixstowe South	66		

Daventry

19:36	4O92	Daventry - Dollands Moor	92	WFO	(to Novara)

Dollands Moor

21:40	4L06	Eurotunnel Boundary - Ripple Lane	92	THO	(runs from Euro Boundary)
22:15	4M90	Frethun (Calais) - Daventry	92	MWFO	(ex Novara)

Doncaster Railport

22:59	4L35	Doncaster Railport - Felixstowe South	66		

Felixstowe

10:45	4M23	Felixstowe North - Hams Hall	66		
11:20	4E33	Felixstowe South - Doncaster	66		
17:20	4M02	Felixstowe South - Hams Hall	66		
01:48	4E78	Felixstowe North - Selby	66		
03:23	4M21	Felixstowe North - Hams Hall	66		
04:12	4M29	Felixstowe South - Barton Dock	66		

Hams Hall

15:21	4L22	Hams Hall - Felixstowe North	66		
22:36	4L23	Hams Hall - Felixstowe North	66		
03:55	4L02	Hams Hall - Felixstowe South	66	MX	

Ripple Lane

20:08	4O73	Ripple Lane - Eurotunnel Boundary	66	FO	(runs with '92' DIT)

Selby

11:43	4L78	Selby - Felixstowe North	66	FX	(FO runs to Felixstowe South)

This service used to run via the North London Line (NLL) before being re-routed cross country, including a spell going via the 'GOBLIN' when the NLL was closed for twelve months for extensive remodelling work. On 3rd December 2011, No.66729 'Derby County' (above) approaches Whittlesea station with 4L02, 03:55 Hams Hall - Felixstowe South.

However, on 8th October 2011, 4L02 looks unusually empty, at least immediately behind GBRf / EuroPorte No.66734 (below) when it was observed at Kennett. The 'Up' starter signal is something of a period piece, an example of a type used quite extensively by the LNER, a concrete post bracket signal with a doll of tubular construction - alas now no longer operative as Kennett signal box is now out of use.   **Nick Slocombe (3)**

4L02

The Selby intermodal was the first such train to be operated by GBRf. 'Metronet' Class 66/7 No.66720 'Metronet Pathfinder' (above) passes through Selby with 4L78, 11:43 Selby - Felixstowe. This was the ECML until the 'Selby Diversion' opened in 1983 between Temple Hirst Jct. and Colton Jct.   **Ian Ball**

(Opposite) : The crossing instructions are plainly clear for all who wish to cross the line at Hayfield, which is just east of Bessacarr on the Lincoln line. On 23rd March, 'Barbie'-liveried No.66723 'Chinook' approaches with 4L78, diverted off the ECML due to engineering work. Cantle water tower is on the horizon.

Meanwhile, GBRf Europorte-liveried No.66730 'Whitemoor' (below) trundles along the 'Up Lincoln / Down Loco' single line from Black Carr Junction to join the Lincoln line at Bessacarr Junction, Doncaster, on 29th February with the diverted 4L78 intermodal.   **Alan Padley (2)**

4L78

4073 :

No.66719 'Metro-land' (left) shines in the afternoon sun at Redhill with an extremely late running and diverted 4073, 20:08 Ripple Lane - Dollands Moor intermodal, formed of refrigerated containers, which are nicknamed 'Reefers'.

This is a seasonal service and the balancing move for the inward service (4L06) from Valencia (see page 13).

Alan Hazelden

Inter-Continental Intermodal

4M90 : A Container shipper, DFDS, is one of the first to sign a contract with GBRf and Europorte Channel to haul a mixed goods multi-modal train from Daventry through the Channel Tunnel to France and then on to Novara in Northern Italy.

On 15th July 2011, No.92032 (above) powers past Soulbury, on the northern outskirts of Leighton Buzzard, with the retimed 4M90, 09:47 Dollands Moor - Daventry, formed of Norfolk Line 'curtainsiders'.

Class 92 No.92032 and Class 66/7 No.66731 became the first locos in the fleet to receive new corporate colours, following the tie up between GBRf and Europorte.

Nigel Gibbs

Felixstowe - Hams Hall

'Metronet' Class 66/7, No.66718 'Gwyneth Dunwoody' (above) powers out of Felixstowe North terminal with 4M23, the 10:43 Felixstowe North - Hams Hall service; some of the dockside cranes can be seen protruding above the tree-line. **James Welham**

4M23 was one of GBRf's first Hams Hall 'landbridge' services and, along with 4M02, is routed via the North London Line; others run via Bury St Edmunds, Ely and Leicester as gauge enhancements now allow large containers on standard flats over the Fens. Taken from Highbury & Islington, No.66706 (below) passes what used to be Canonbury West Junction on 16th April 2011 with a fully laden 4M23 - note the different size boxes. **Nick Slocombe**

4M29 : At 08:21hrs, 15th October 2011, No.66712 'Peterborough Power Signalbox' (above) passes Ely with GBRf's new 4M29, 04:12 Felixstowe South – Barton Dock intermodal; the cows, seemingly unconcerned by the train, are more intent on watching the photographer!
Nick Slocombe

4L06 : A colourful combination sees Rainbow Warrior' Class 66/7 No.66720 + Class 92 No.92032 (below) approach Fen Pond Lane road bridge, Ightam, on 16th December 2011 on a late running 4L06, 21:30 Dollands Moor – Ripple Lane intermodal. 4L06 is booked to run with this traction arrangement, but is normally an overnight train, which will be routed via the CTRL at some point in the future. This train service brings in fruit from Valencia, Spain, in refrigerated containers.
Alan Hazelden

66709

On 25th April, GB Railfreight name Class 66/7 loco 'Sorrento' to honour the 10 year partnership with Mediterranean Shipping Company (MSC).

The newly liveried loco, No.66709, is unveiled at a special ceremony at the Port of Felixstowe, where GBRf has its Intermodal headquarters, by GBRf Managing Director John Smith and Maurizio Aponte, Director of MSC Europe.

John Smith commented: "It is an honour to name this locomotive Sorrento to celebrate the 10-year partnership between MSC and GBRf".... Dan Everitt, Managing Director of MSC UK, added:

"MSC is proud to unveil the newly liveried locomotive to celebrate our 10 year partnership with GB Railfreight, as it also provides us with an opportunity to highlight our commitment to investment in rail services. Last year, we moved over 100,000 containers by rail, which we estimate was almost 20% of the Port of Felixstowe's total rail moves."

(above & below) : No.66709 'Sorrento' stands on the quayside at Felixstowe after being named. The embellishment of a MSC container ship on the body side is superb and certainly does not look out of place - will this loco be restricted to just intermodal traffic or will it see use elsewhere?

The loco previously carried MSC 'Medite' black livery, applied in July 2002 to mark GBRf's expansion of the Hams Hall and Selby services going over to daily running. At the same time, No66709 was named 'Joseph Arnold Davies' after the father of Medite's Managing Director, Roy Davies.

No.66709 leaves Felixstowe after the naming ceremony DIT behind No.66743 on 4M02, the 17:20 Felixstowe South - Hams Hall service.

MSC & the Port of Felixstowe

MSC (Mediterranean Shipping Company) of Geneva, Switzerland, is a privately owned shipping line, founded in 1970, growing rapidly from a small conventional ship operator to one of the leading global shipping lines of the world. It's maritime fleet has expanded to over 450 vessels, over 350 of which being container ships.

MSC operates through the Port of Felixstowe and GBRf is the railfreight operator responsible for transporting containers on a daily basis to & from terminals at Barton Dock, Doncaster, Hams Hall and Selby.

The Port of Felixstowe, Suffolk, is the UK's busiest container port, dealing with 35% of the country's container cargo. It was developed following the abandonment of a project for a deep-water harbour at Maplin Sands.

(Above) : This is a view of the bay, where the rivers Orwell and Stour empty into the North Sea. While MV 'Mare Lycium' is berthed at the Trinity terminal, MV 'MSC Emma' is being turned ready for berthing.

(Below) : This is an example of one of the many MSC container ships - MV 'MSC Michaela' - prior to berthing at Felixstowe. This particular vessel was built in 2002, is 997ft in length and has a gross tonnage of 73,819. It's call sign is 'HOEZ' and sails under the flag of Panama. **Michael Davies (4)**

Teigngrace Comes on Stream

Kronsopan at Chirk are supplementing their existing supplies of timber from Carlisle (6J37) and, occasionally, Ribblehead (6Z41) with a new flow from Teigngrace in Devon, which is a welcome boost for freight traffic in the South West. Teigngrace is situated on the former 3 miles 50 chains long branch which runs from Newton Abbott to Heathfield. The new flow runs as:

6Z53, (ThO) 14:41 Teigngrace - Chirk   Colas 66

On 19th April, Colas Rail Class 66/8 No.66745 (above) races through Dawlish with 6Z53, the 14.41 Teigngrace - Chirk formed of 15 converted 'KFA' timber wagons.   **Peter Slater**

Class 66/8 No.66847 sets off from Chirk (6Z41) on 1st December 2011 hauling a rake of 'KFA' timber carriers to collect the first loaded train of timber. The train stages overnight at Gloucester and goes forward to Teigngrace the following day (6Z50). The 'KFAs' are:

GERS 97221	GERS 97216	GERS 97168	GERS 97158	GERS 97162
GERS 97112	GERS 97153	GERS 97235	GERS 97268	GERS 97106
GERS 97166	GERS 97229	GERS 97147	GERS 97247	

Route & Times

6Z53, Teigngrace - Chirk

TEIGNGRACE	**14:41**	Newton Abbot	15:06 - 15:26	Teignmouth	15:33
Dawlish	15:36	Exeter St Davids	15:48	Tiverton Parkway	16:07
Whiteball	16:11	Taunton	16:22	Cogload Jct	16:27
Bridgewater	16:34	Uphill Jct	16:48	Worle Jct	16:56
Bristol T. Meads	17:34	Dr Days Jct	17:36	Pilning	17:53
Severn Tunnel Jct	18:03	Maindee East Jct	18:36	Maindee North Jct	18:38
Abervagenny	19:42	Pontrilas	19:57	Hereford	20:15
Leominster	20:34	Craven Arms	20:54	Shrewsbury	21:20
Nantwich	21:53	Gresty Lane	21:59	Crewe	22:02
Chester	22:34	Wrexham	23:03	**CHIRK**	**23:45**

Class 66/8, No 66745 (above) reaches the summit of Llanvihangel Bank, north of Abergavenny, with 6Z41, the 09.13 Chirk - Teigngrace empty logs carriers on 19th March. The train is heading straight to Devon from the Kronsopan plant because the wagons had been used the previous weekend. Normally, they head south earlier and stable at Gloucester over the weekend to await their next turn of duty.   **Peter Slater**

(Overleaf) : On Wednesday, 11th January, No66847 (Page 18) is seen again, this time heading along the banks of the River Teign near Bishopsteignton hauling 6Z51, 14:41 Teigngrace - Chirk loaded timber.

On Tuesday, 21st February, No.66745 (below) passes the timber pile at Teigngrace Crossing, while working 6Z50, 08:36 Gloucester New Yard - Teigngrace, which had run via Heathfield to run round. The branch line from Newton Abbott was once the Moretonhampstead & South Devon Railway, which closed to passenger trains on 28 February 1959.   **Robert Sherwood (2)**

The 'Eco Express'

Green Pioneers GBRf initially moved into the Biomass market in January 2011 after successful trials, running three trains from Tyne Dock to Drax power station, followed by a trial working out of Avonmouth in October 2011.

The Avonmouth flow soon moved (for operational reasons?) to Portbury in February, although large stockpiles of biomass could be seen at times on land adjacent to Bennett's Sidings at Avonmouth and West Wharf. The loaded train originally left Portbury at 04:23hrs, but settled down to run as::

       6E95, 22:33 (Q) Portbury - Drax   **2 x GBRf Class 66s**

As the Portbury train runs overnight, photographic opportunities are restricted to the return empties, which run in sociable hours. A further bonus is that both services run with double-headed Class 66s to enable the loaded train to ascend the Lickey Incline without the need of a banking loco. DBS normally provide a banking loco in the shape of a Class 66/0, but this is not available for other operators without incurring additional running costs.

The first train out of Portbury runs on 18th February hauled by No.66723 *'Chinook'* + No.66706 *'Nene Valley'* and the consist of 'IIAs', which are specially converted 'HYA' wagons, which have automated top and bottom doors, is the following formation:

70.6955.284-4	70.6955.272-9	70.6955.244-8	70.6955.250-5	70.6955.264-6
70.6955.260-4	70.6955.270-3	70.6955.268-7	70.6955.255-4	70.6955.252-1
70.6955.265-3	70.6955.263-8	70.6955.271-1	70.6955.245-5	70.6955.254-7
70.6955.247-1	70.6955.259-6	70.6955.256-2	70.6955.253-9	70.6955.261-2

GBRf Class No.66709 'Joseph Arnold Davies' + No.66715 'Valour ...' (above) approach Hexthorpe Junction on 20th February with 4V94, Drax - Portbury biomass empties. The train has come via Doncaster station, South Yorkshire Junction and St. James Junction; the double track to the left is the station avoiding line from Bentley Junction and the lines to the right lead to Bridge Junction.

(Previous Page) : During April, GBRf's 'Rainbow Warrior' Class 66/7 No.66720 makes several sorties on the new Drax biomass flow paired with No.66727 'Andrew Scott CBE' and the two '66/7s' are seen on 19th April powering 4V64, 10:12 Doncaster Roberts Road - Portbury through a wet Mexborough station. Mexborough is situated on the Swinton - Doncaster line, seven miles west of Doncaster. **Alan Padley (2)**

Ex-Freightliner Class 66/5 liveried No.66738 + No.66709 'Joseph Arnold Davies' (above) approach the Portbury Dock stopboard with 4V94, 09.52 Doncaster Decoy Yard - Portbury Docks empty biomass Hoppers on Thursday, 23rd February. As we will see later in this issue, this is the last time we shall see No.66709 in the distinctive 'Medite' black livery.

On 25th July, No.66737 'Lesia' (below) sweeps round the curve at Yate in charge of 4V94, 10.12 Doncaster Roberts Road - Portbury Docks biomass empties. Due to the derailment of No.66734 on 28th June, while working 6S45, North Blyth - Fort William loaded 'alcan' alumina tanks, alongside Loch Trieg on the WHL, GBRf is one Class 66/7 short. Consequently, the biomass service is now running as a single loco and the returning full train now runs via Oxford instead of the Lickey incline.   **Chris Perkins (2)**

The Tesco train is certainly an impressive sight, as we can see here. DRS Class 66/4 No.66429 (above) skirts the River Severn at Gatcombe on 25th March with 4V38, 07:57 Daventry - Cardiff Wentloog intermodal.

Steven King

4V38 The Gloucester - Chepstow line is a very popular line with photographers and this striking image depicts No.66428 (below) powering the new 4V38, 07:57 Daventry - Cardiff Wentloog 'Tesco Express' intermodal at Thornwell on St. David's Day, 1st March.

Jamie Squibbs

More 'Less CO2' Expresses

In February, supermarket giant Tesco launch a new 'Tesco Express' to Wentloog FLT in South Wales to complement a service to Thurrock (4L48 / 4M77). The Welsh train is coded:

4V38, 07:57	Daventry - Cardiff Wentloog	**DRS Class 66/4**
4M46, 00:47	Cardiff Wentloog - Daventry	**DRS Class 66/4**

The Wentloog trains run seven days a week and the above departure times relate to the Monday - Saturday operation. Tesco reckon the Wentloog and Thurrock services will save 40,000 lorry journeys a year and this expansion demonstrates Tesco's committment to rail; they already run trains from Daventry to Scotland and between Mossend and Inverness.

Trains leaving from Daventry will transport products such as shampoo, deodorants, confectionary and wine. Trains returning to Daventry will be loaded with items such as washing powder, washing up liquid, and detergent from Proctor & Gamble.

The Wentloog train is particularly interesting as this is the first time intermodal traffic has run on the Cheltenham - Birmingham main line and affords great photographic opportunities on the scenic stretch between Gloucester and Severn Tunnel Junction, as we will see.

The trains are branded 'Less CO2 Rail' and the inaugural Wentloog flow runs as:

4V38, 08:22 Daventry - Wentloog   28th February

Location	Timings
Daventry	08:22
Rugby	08:33
Nuneaton	08:52
Water Orton	09:21
Landor Street	09:30
Barnt Green	09:53
Cheltenham	10:37
Gloucester	10:52
Chepstow	11:21
Severn T. Jct.	11:30
Newport	11:49
Wentloog	12:02

Consist:

70.4901.020-0	IDA
70.4901.016-8	IDA
70.4901.014-3	IDA
70.4901.009-3	IDA
70.4901.011-9	IDA
70.4901.021-8	IDA
68.4909.067-3	IKA
68.4909.871-8	IKA
68.4909.134-1	IKA
68.4909.021-0	IKA

On 15th April, Class 66/4 No.66429 (above) is allocated to 4V38, Daventry - Wentloog Intermodal and is seen passing Saltley, heading for Landor Street and the Birmingham New Street avoider to take it to Kings Norton and then the run down the 'Lickey'. **David Weake**

(Overleaf) : On 5th March, No.66434 (in newly branded 'Malcolm' livery) heads 4V38 and passes Portskewett, near Caldicot, where the M48 Severn Bridge can be seen in the background. **Peter Slater**

Lynemouth Smelter Closes

Northumberland's biggest private employer closes with the loss of over 500 jobs ....
Rio Tinto Alcan's aluminium smelter at Lynemouth shuts its hot metal section on 29th March.

Some operational activity in the smelter's carbon and casting plants, which currently employ around 200 staff, will continue until later in the year, and a team of around 60 employees will remain on site beyond the closure of all operations to work on decommissioning and remediation.

The last local Alcan trip runs on Wednesday, 21st March, hauled by GBRf Class 66/7 No.66727 'Andrew Scott CBE' and, for the record, here is a reminder of the local alcan 'trip':

> 6N70, 06:35 Lynemouth - North Blyth   empty 'PCA's
> 6N64, 15:13 North Blyth - Lynemouth   loaded 'PCA' alumina tanks

The nearby Lynemouth power station will continue to receive and burn coal until 2014, when it is scheduled to close for conversion to biomass fuel. It is likely biomass will be imported through the port of Blyth and there are plans to build a biomass power station at Battleship Wharf, Blyth. Raw materials for Alcan will continue to be shipped in to Blyth for, perhaps, another two years and moved by rail (train 6S45) to Lochaber.

An image of the final 'trip' from North Blyth is included here along with a couple of other shots to record the passing of GBRf 66/s on this now defunct flow - RIP!

The Final Journey .... 21st March and GBRf 'Barbie' liveried Class 66/7 No.66727 'Andrew Scott CBE' (above) departs the import terminal at North Blyth with loaded 'PCA' alumina tanks for the FINAL TIME on the LAST EVER 'trip': 6N64, 15:13 North Blyth - Lynemouth.

(Previous Page) :

On a sunny, Friday, 24th February, Europorte GBRF liveried Class 66/7 No.66733 passes Cambois with another 6N64, 15:13 North Blyth - Lynemouth 'trip' of alumina. Two wind turbines can be seen in the North Sea, half-a-mile off the Northumberland coast, constructed in 2000. Eight years previously, nine wind turbines were constructed along Blyth Harbour's East Pier in 1992, some of which can be seen on the extreme right of this image.

After the hype of the 'Deltic' of 2011, nothing else of interest could possibly fall onto the Alcan trips ......
then up pops ex-Colas Rail liveried Class 66/7 No.66742. On 13th January No.66742 (above), recently
transferred to GBRf, passes Freemans Crossing on 6N64, 15:13 North Blyth - Lynemouth loaded alumina
tanks. Freemans Crossing is possibly the best known photographic location on the 'Blyth & Tyne' network.

Of course, the semaphores in this remote part of the 'Blyth & Tyne' network are an added bonus for any
composition as shown here in this view, No.66729 'Derby County' (below) passing Marcheys House on a
Saturday in charge of 6N58, 08.00 North Blyth - Lynemouth Alcan 'trip'.   **Martin Cook (4)**

DCR take on Shipley Scrap

Devon & Cornwall Railways (DCR) move into the freight market in March moving scrap metal from Crossley Evans scrapyard in Shipley to Cardiff Tidal, previously operated by DBS.

6Z56, (ThO) 17:44 Shipley - Cardiff Tidal   DCR Class 56

DCR operate this flow using Class 56s, running singularly or in pairs, and a rake of 'JRA' bogie box wagons - more 'grid' power on the main line, which will not go amiss!

DCR TIMELINE

DCR are keen to expand their loco 'spot-hire' business and here is a summary of their 'grid' activity leading up to the launch of the Shipley flow:

2011

9th December : DCR purchase two further Class 56s - No.56091 and No.56103.

1st December : No.56311 works a special, 6Z61, Parkeston Quay - Kingsbury, taking 18 'TUA' Carless 'Mud Oil' 2-axle tanks for scrapping at EMR, Kingsbury, now that the Aberdeen 'Mud Oil' train has ceased and the wagons are surplus to requirements.

22nd December : No.56311 works a 4Z56, Marcroft Engineering (Stoke) - Motherwell, moving a rake of 1999-built 'IKA' 'Megafret' wagons, owned by Swiss leasing company AAE.

24th December : No.56312 is outshopped, still in grey livery, but with branding to advertise 'Railfest 2012', which is taking place at the National Railway Museum (York) in June. DCR will support the event by providing Class 56s to haul exhibits to York.

2012

2nd February : No.56312 collects No.56091 from Bescot Yard and takes it to Washwood Heath before venturing to Barrow Hill to collect No.56303, which had been on load bank testing.

27th / 28th February : DCR hire No.56302 from Nemesis Rail and moves 'JRAs between Wembley - Cardiff Tidal - Burton on Trent, in preparation for the Shipley scrap train.

14th March : No.56302, still on hire to DCR, works route familiarisation trips:

0Z56, 04:00 Burton Wetmore Sidings - Shipley .... 0Z57 return

15th March : No.56302 arrives from Burton (6Z69) with 'JRAs to form the inaugural 6Z56 service to Cardiff Tidal - the train finally leaves on Saturday, 17th March, running as 6Z70.

Dark clouds threaten, but just enough sunshine prevails to record a 'grid' working in Yorkshire. Class 56/3 No.56302 (above) passes Killamarsh on 18th March with the loaded scrap train, running on this day as 6Z70, Shipley - Cardiff Tidal. Killamarsh is on the 'Old Road', which bypasses the bottleneck of Sheffield Midland, and links Rotherham (Masborough Station Junction) and Chesterfield (Tapton Junction). **Ross Byers**

Just like old times, a Class 56 working a heavy freight train on the busy four track stretch of the main line between Colton Junction and Church Fenton. On 17th April, No.56312 (bottom left) looks impressive as it passes Bolton Percy Nature Reserve with 6Z56, the 10:15 Stockton - Cardiff Tidal scrap train. During this time, 6Z56 often alternates between Shipley and Stockton scrapyards. **Neil Harvey**

On 14th April, No. 56312 is out again, but this time playing second fiddle to Class 47 No.47812 (below), which is seen piling on the power through Saltley, Birmingham, with 6Z56, Cardiff Tidal - Stockton. St. Andrews, home to Birmingham City Football Club, can be seen on the skyline. **David Weake**

6Z56

After months of 'grid' activity involving DCR's No.56311 and No.56312 on the Shipley scrap metal service, enthusiasts are greeted in August by the debut appearance of No.56303, resplendent in green livery and sporting the name 'Brian' on the body side.

In preparation for the next trainload of scrap metal, No.56303 (above) heads north through Oakenshaw, on the outskirts of Wakefield, with 6Z56, the 11:05 Chaddesden - Shipley empty scrap. The 'JRAs' have been into Pullman Rail works at Cardiff Canton recently and been strengthened by the addition of an all-round trim added to the top of each wagon. The date of this image is 22nd August. **Neil Harvey**

With the City of Wakefield in the background, No.56311 (above) passes Oakenshaw with 6Z56, the 13:48 Shipley Crossley Evans - Cardiff loaded scrap on 25th May 2012. The single line on the left of view leads from Oakenshaw Junction to Oakenshaw South Junction, which was the former Midland Main Line from Leeds to Sheffield via Normanton and Royston. This short section is now all that remains and, although used for occasional testing and driver training, it has remained open for the once or twice weekly sand train destined for the Monk Bretton glassworks.   **Mark Walker**

Back again with No.56303 on 28th August and what a super sight (and sound, no doubt!) as No.56303 (below) accelerates up the 1 in 160 grade past Shay lane (Crofton) towards Hare Park Junction with a fully loaded 6Z56, the 13:14 Shipley Crossley Evans - Cardiff Tidal scrap.   **Richard Armstrong**

DCR Spot Hire
Peak Forest 'Grid'

Due to a shortage of locos and/or train crews, DBS turn to Devon & Cornwall Railways (DCR) who provide two Class 56s to work stone trains from Peak Forest to Stourton (Leeds) and Attercliffe Road (Sheffield).

Unfortunately, the loaded trains do not run during sociable hours from a photographic point of view, but we do have a record of the first working from Peak Forest on 17th July - a rare event not to be missed!

Services :

6Z17, 19:54 Peak Forest - Stourton

6Z19, 20:32 Peak Forest - Attercliffe Rd

Consist :

The initial service runs to Attercliffe Road using a rake of 19 'JRAs':

Carkind : JRA	Design Code : P0177M		Pool : 732	
70.6790.095-7	70.6790.051-0	70.6790.043-7	70.6790.049-4	70.6790.061-9
70.6790.094-0	70.6790.096-5	70.6790.030-4	70.6790.065-0	70.6790.059-3
70.6790.031-2	70.6790.062-7	70.6790.058-5	70.6790.082-5	70.6790.064-3
70.6790.033-8	70.6790.085-8	70.6790.067-6	70.6790.060-1	

In readiness for this work, route learning takes place on 14th July. No.56311 works 0Z11, the 08:55 Derby - Derby, routed via Chesterfield, Grindleford, Edale, Peak Forest, Sheffield, Thrybergh Junction, Sheffield - Chesterfield. No.56311 returns light engine from Derby to Washwood Heath and is swapped for No.56312, which takes over the route learning between Derby and Peak Forest.

Selective Images

Awaiting the Off : DCR Class 56s No.56311 + 56312 (top left) idle away atop their rake of 19 'JRAs' bound for Attercliffe Road, Sheffield. You cannot fail but notice the start of a new steel structure being erected on the left adjacent to the '56s' - another abomination to mar the aesthetics!

Making Up : The 'JRAs' have been moved out of the loading area at Dove Holes quarry into the siding and now the two '56s' (bottom left) can do no more than bide their time. Note, 'JRAs' are used on the Attercliffe Road flow, while the Stourton flow utilises 'HOA' and 'IIA' bogie hoppers owned by DBS.

And They're Off! : Finally, it's time to go and Nos.56311 + 56312 (above) pile on the power as they accelerate past Peak Forest signal box and away with 6Z56, the 20:32 Peak Forest - Attercliffe Road stone. Two DBS Class 66/0s and a solitary Class 60 can be seen stabled in the holding sidings.   **Colin Dixon (3)**

6M11 : Storm clouds gather overhead as DCR Class 56s No.56311 + 56303 (above) head north past Clay Cross on 10th September with 6M11, (MWFO) 10:00 Washwood Heath - Peak Forest empty bogie stone hoppers. This is a DBS-operated train, but sub-contracted to DCR for motive power and crew.   **Alan Padley**

6M08 : Colas 'grid' No.56094 (below) powers past Ogden's Wood (Gonerby Moor) on 7th September in charge of 6M08, (WX) 17:20 Boston-Washwood Heath steel, formed of eight 'IHA' canvas-sided steel carriers, in some rather nice evening light. The location for this excellent image is near to Barkston East Junction, which is where the line to Grantham and the ECML diverges from the Sleaford - Ancaster - Bottesford - Nottingham main line.   **Richard Armstrong**

Boston Steel goes '56'

Freight operator Colas Rail purchase four Class 56s, all from the remainder of the locos recently sold by DB Schenker. These are Nos.

56087

56094

56105

56113

These join the Colas fleet and move from Crewe TMD to Washwood Heath for repairs.

This takes the Colas fleet to 12 locos of Class 47, 56 and 66.

No.56094 is the first '56' to be repainted in the elegant Colas Rail colours and is put to work straightaway on the Boston Docks steel flow, which has now seen all three types of Colas traction on this service:

6M08, (ThO) 17:20 Boston Docks - Washwood Heath

The Colas '56s' will become regular traction on this flow.

On a wet and miserable 7th June, the Class 56 and Class 47/7 combination are out working together again and No.56094 + No.47739 (above) pass through Attenborough with 6E07, 11:51 Washwood Heath - Boston Docks steel empties; the onlooker presumably doesn't mind getting drenched to witness this fine sight. Attenborough is on the main line to Nottingham, 2-miles from Trent Junction. **Alan Padley**

(Overleaf) : The first time the Colas Rail liveried Class 56 - No.56094 - makes its debut appearance is 25th May and photographers are out in force to witness the event - they are not to be disappointed. Enclosed in woodland near Weston on Trent, No.56094 ambles along the Sheet Stores branch with 6E07, 11:51 Washwood Heath - Boston Docks formed of canvas-sided 'IHAs'. The 56 only runs as far as Mansfield Junction (due to 'operational' issues!) and so Class 47 No.47739 'Robin of Templecombe' continues from there on its own. **Alan Hazelden**

Boston Docks Traction

In March, Colas Class 66/8s start to replace the tried and trusted '47/7s', which in turn are being ousted by refurbished Class 56s.

Class 66/8 No.66848 (top right) passes Saxondale on 6th March with 6E07, 11:51 Washwood Heath - Boston Docks steel empties, the train mid-way between Radcliffe on Trent and Bingham, on the Nottingham - Sleaford / Grantham line. Note the telescopic steel sided 'IHA' steel carriers which also now appear on this flow.   **Mick Tindall**

Here is the new order; Class 56 No.56094 (centre) is seen passing Chellaston, between Stenson Jct. - Sheet Stores Jct. on 23rd July with 6E07, 11.51 Washwood Heath - Boston Docks.   **Nigel Gibbs**

Finally, the Colas 47, which has been the prime motive power to and from Boston Docks for a long time.

Class 47/7 No.47727 'Rebecca' (below) passes the picturesque ex-Great Northern Railway signal box at Ancaster, opened circa 1873, with 6E07.   **Mick Tindall**

Redcar Limestone

As reported in the previous issue of 'Loco Review', steel production has resumed at Redcar steelworks, albeit restricted to steel for the export market at present. The blast furnaces need to be lined with limestone for this purpose and trainloads are being brought in from Dowlow, Rylstone and Shap Quarry, plus Dolomite from nearby Thrislington.

The respective services are:

6Z67,	(MFX)	08:42	Thrislington - Redcar	F.Liner 66	Dolomite**
6Z16,	(MO)	08:31	Carlisle Yard - Redcar	F.Liner 66	Limestone
6E59,	(TThO)	20:52	Dowlow - Redcar	DBS 66	Limestone
6Z65,	(TThO)	23:11	Rylstone - Redcar	DBS 66	Limestone *

* The Rylstone service operates as a 'STP' flow which means the headcode and pathing will vary from week to week. Sometimes it will use the path / wagons off the Rylstone - Hull Dairycoates train, in which case it tends to depart Rylstone at 03:53hrs, or it can use the set of wagons off the Dowlow flow, when it will depart earlier.

** Dolomite is a carbonate mineral composed of calcium magnesium carbonate - chemical formula $CaMg(CO_3)_2$ - which is needed in the steel making process to protect the refractory lining of the steel furnace or converter, increasing the life span — a crucial parameter from a financial viewpoint.

Here, DBS 'shed' No.66186 (above) passes Copmanthorpe on the ECML, 30th May, with 4Z67, the 09:30 (MTX) Redcar - Dowlow (Brigg Sidings) empty limestone hoppers. This train is the return diagram of the loaded 6E59, 20:52 Dowlow - Redcar which comprises a mix of hoppers, including former EWS-branded and Cemex-branded 'HOA' hoppers and 'IIAs'. **Carl Gorse**

No.66613 (top right) is seen passing Tow Top, Cowran, mid-way between Wetheral and Brampton on the Tyne Valley line with the delayed 6Z16, 08:31 (MFO) Carlisle Yard - Redcar loaded limestone. The consist is a mix of green-liveried and white 'HIA' bogie limestone hoppers. **Ian Ball**

FHH No.66602 (bottom right) passes South Bank on 20th June with empty 'HIAs', running as 6Z68, 12:15 Redcar - Thrislington. Part of the huge Lackenby steelworks forms the backdrop. **Alan Padley**

6Z16 ▲   ▼ 6Z68

Colas Go North of the Border

Colas rail expand their freight portfolio by 'cherry picking', if this the appropriate term, taking over some of the Grangemouth aviation fuel oil runs from DB Schenker. So, the striking Colas livery will now be seen in Scotland for the first time and the respective workings are:

6Z96,	(WO)	21:15 Grangemouth - Sinfin	Colas 66
6Z46,	(TFO)	07:11 Grangemouth - Prestwick	Colas 66
6Z46,	(WO)	07:11 Grangemouth - Linkswood	Colas 66

This is an interesting development as DBS retain the Grangemouth - Dalston flow and used to have a neat operation; the loco off the returning empties (6S36) arriving at Grangemouth would have taken out 6D18, which was the 2-axle 'TTA' fuel oil tanks for either Fort William, Lairg, Linkswood, Prestwick, Riccarton or Sinfin. Later in the evening, a second Class 66 would arrive from Prestwick to work the loaded 6M34, Grangemouth - Dalston, then the same procedure would happen all over again, 6 days per week. Let's see how this new operation pans out.

COLAS INTERNAL 'TRIPS'

6Z46, GRANGEMOUTH - PRESTWICK

Location	Timings
GRANGEMOUTH	**07:11**
Fouldubs Jct	07:26
Grangemouth Jct	07:31
Falkirk Graham St	07:32
Carnuirs East Jct	07:36
Carmuirs West Jct	07:38
Greenhill Lower Jct	07:41
Cumbernauld	07:47
Garnqueen North Jct	07:51
Gartsherrie South Jct	07:54
Coatbridge Central	07:56
Langloan Jct	07:58
Carmyle	08:05
Rutherglen East Jct	08:09
Larkfield Jct	08:15
Terminus Jct	08:17
Shields Jct	08:23
Paisley	08:30
Elderslie	08:33
Dalry	08:53
Kilwinning	08:58
Irvine	09:02
Barassie Jct	09:06
Prestwick	09:11
Newton Jct	09:14
Ayr	09:16 - 09:48
Newton Jct	09:52
Prestwick	09:54
Monkton Ground Frame	09:57 - 10:00
PRESTWICK	**10:05**

6Z46, GRANGEMOUTH - LINKSWOOD

Location	Timings
GRANGEMOUTH	**07:11**
Fouldubs Jct	07:26
Grangemouth Jct	07:31
Falkirk Graham St	07:32
Carnuirs East Jct	07:36
Larbert Jct	07:37
Larbert	07:39
Stirling	07:50
Dunblane	07:57
Blackford	08:12
Hilton Jct	08:28
Perth Dundee Loop	08:31 - 08:46
Perth	08:48
Errol	09:07
Dundee Central Jct	09:24
Dundee Holding Sidings	09:29 - 09:30
Dundee West	09:35 - 10:32
Dundee Holding Sidings	10:37 - 10:38
Dundee Central Jct	10:43
Tay Bridgew South	10:51
LINKSWOOD	**11:03**

COLAS RAIL FREIGHT

Craig Adamson

After the new flows settle in, the reporting codes change to 6M65 (Sinfin), 6R46 (Prestwick) and 6L82 (Linkswood).

On 5th September, having completed a reversal at Dundee, No.66850 (above) continues on the last leg of its journey to Linkswood and is seen crossing the Tay Bridge with 6L82, 07:42 Grangemouth - Linkswood aviation fuel.

The train will return to Grangemouth via Ladybank - Thornton - Dunfermline - Kincardine - Alloa - Stirling - Larbert - Falkirk Grahamston - Grangemouth Junction.   **Jim Ramsay**

A week after inception, No.66847 (below) powers away from Larbert Junction on 9th May with 6Z46, the 07:11 Grangemouth - Linkswood fuel oil tanks, formed of the colourful green liveried 2-axle 'TTA' tank wagons. A splash of black, orange and yellow is a very welcome addition to the Scottish freight scene.

The 'Falkirk Wheel' is also in shot, above the rear cab of the loco. This is a rotating boat lift used to connect the Forth and Clyde Canal with the Union Canal. The lift opened in 2002 and the two canals were previously connected by a series of 11 locks which, by the 1930's, had fallen into disuse.   **Guy Houston**

Having worked into Grangemouth with oil trains, No.47739 'Robin of Templecombe' and No.66847 (above) sit in the sunshine next to a track machine (No.DR73932) on a sunny and hazy 20th May at Stirling middle. The locos for this traffic stable at Stirling and run to and from Grangemouth, typically:

    0Z46, 05:59 Stirling - Grangemouth

    0Z47, 20:54 Grangemouth - Stirling

It's 17th May, half-past eight in the evening, pouring with rain and not the ideal time to be out taking photos of moving trains, but a Colas 47 on a rake of green tanks in Scotland is not an everyday occurrence! Running an hour late, No.47739 'Robin of Templecombe' (below) rounds the curve at Carmuirs with 6Z47, the 16:56 Prestwick - Grangemouth empty 'TTA' tanks - ISO 4000 needed for the shot! **Guy Houston (2)**

Colas Rail Freight's No.66850 (above) runs along the shoreline at Invergowrie Bay on the approach to Dundee on Wednesday, 15th July, with the Grangemouth - Linkswood loaded aviation fuel tanks for RAF Leuchars. The train still leaves Grangemouth at 07:11hrs, but is now re-coded 6Z82.   **Jim Ramsay**

(Overleaf) : On 1st May, No.66847 works the first train of aviation fuel for RAF Leuchars and, on the return journey   the following day, No.66847 crosses the magnificent Linlithgow viaduct, with 6Z47, the 14:48 Linkswood - Grangemouth. Linlithgow viaduct was constructed in 1840 to span the River Avon valley and carries the main railway line between Glasgow Queen Street and Edinburgh Waverley. **Alastair Blackwood**

The return empties from Linkswood have similarly been re-coded and No.66850 (below) is seen deep in Fife at Cupar on 25th July with 6Z83, the 14:48 Linkswood - Grangemouth.   **Jim Ramsay**

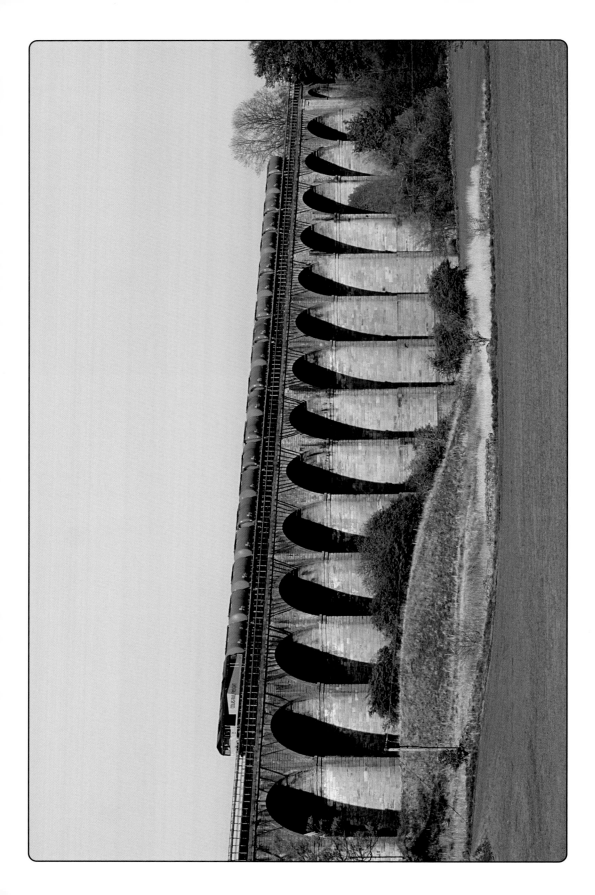

GBRf 'Crossrail' Spoil Trains

'Crossrail' is a major new railway link being built under central London, the first of two routes which are the responsibility of Crossrail Ltd, the other being a proposed Chelsea – Hackney line. It is based entirely on a new main line gauge, using tunnels from Paddington in the west to beyond Whitechapel in the east. The company, Cross London Rail Links, now known as Crossrail Ltd was formed in 2001 to deliver the scheme. The project was approved in October 2007, and the Crossrail Act received Royal Assent in July 2008.

Ten-car trains will run at frequencies of up to 24 trains per hour in each direction through the central tunnel section, planned for commissioning in 2018!

First Trainload leaves .... Friday, 11th May .... 13 wagons leave Crossrail's Westbourne Park site for Northfleet after being loaded with 492 tonnes of earth - train locos are Class 66/7s No.66729 'Derby County' and No.66744, running in 'top and tail' formation. Over the next six weeks, two trains a week will run a return journey between Crossrail's tunnel entrance near Paddington and Northfleet. Later in the summer, train sizes should increase to 27 wagons, running three times a day. At the peak of tunnelling up to five freight trains a day will operate from Westbourne Park carrying a total of 7,000 tonnes of earth.

From Northfleet, the material will be transferred by ship to regeneration sites, including a new RSPB nature reserve at Wallasea Island, Essex. More than 1 million tonnes of earth will be excavated during the tunnelling construction of Crossrail's 6.4km western tunnels between the Royal Oak portal and Farringdon station. The initial train is:

6O88, 09:20 Paddington - Northfleet   **2 x GBRf Class 66/s (T 'n' T)**

(Left) :

Two GBRf Class 66/7s No.66711 and No.66714 'Cromer Lifeboat' stroll through Dartford in top 'n' tail mode with 6O92, the 14:07 Paddington Crossrail - Northfleet spoil train on 20th July.

This train consists of 12 'JNA' bogie box wagons. of which the leading five wagons are empty.

(Previous page) :

GBRf Class 66/7 No.66729 'Derby County' stands alongside the quay at Northfleet (ex-Lafarge site) on 27th April, with 6Z94, Tonbridge - Northfleet (Crossrail) trial spoil train.

On the River Thames, looking across to Tilbury, the MV 'Asperity' makes her way up the river; the vessel is a double-hull oil tanker built in 1997 by Singmarine Pte Ltd and has a gross weight of 2,965 tonnes.

Ian Cuthbertson (2)

On 30th May, GBRf Class 66/7s No.66720 and No.66719 'METRO-LAND' (above) work 6O88, 09:20 Paddington - Northfleet into the Crossrail sidings with the first 'day time' spoil train. These trains will run top 'n' tail for operating purposes and increase in number as the project progresses. The spoil is destined for a large wildlife reserve at Wallasea Island, eight miles north of Southend-on-Sea in Essex, and will be the largest and most important coastal habitat creation scheme in the UK. **Ian Cuthbertson**

Northfleet Rail Revival

1Z65, London Victoria - Northfleet

On 21st June, Thames Gateway Minister, Mr Bob Neill, officially opens the £13.5 million freight link from the North Kent Line to the former Lafarge cement works at Northfleet. To bring invited guests to the opening, GBRf lay on a special from London Victoria using GBRf locos No.66744 and No.73205 'Jeanette', top 'n' tailing six Riviera Mark 1 coaches. In miserable weather, No.66744 (above), suitably adorned with headboard, rolls past Factory Junction and into Wandsworth Road with the special train. **Alan Hazelden (2)**

Ditton - Tees Dock
DRS '57s'

A new DRS-operated intermodal service started running in October 2011, using Class 66/4 traction, conveying chemical products between Ditton and Tees Dock in distinctive yellow 'P & O Ferrymasters' containers on 'IDA' Intermodal Twin Container Wagons.

4M51, 16:10 Tees Dock - Ditton   4E46, 03:43 Ditton - Tees Dock

IDAs :   70.4901.008-5   70.4901.007-7   70.4901.006-9   70.4901.013-5

However, in order to release '66/4s' for other duties, DRS allocate Class 57s for this flow from Monday, 16th July, running singularly or in pairs - a welcome addition of heritage DRS traction on non-flask work. Also, on most Saturdays, this service runs via Carlisle and the Tyne Valley.

(Above) : On Thursday, 2nd August, Class 57 No.57009 passes Colton Junction heading 4E38, 03:43 (TThO) Ditton - Tees Dock intermodal which takes a takes a circuitous route via the WCML, Midland Main Line and and eventually up the East Coast Main Line. This is the only regular DRS operated freight through York but even this sometimes runs via the WCML and the Tyne Valley instead.   **Derek Holmes**

Routing & Passing Times

4M51, 16:10 Tees Dock - Ditton

Tees Dock	**16:10**	Grangetown	16:19	South Bank	16:27
Middlesbrough	16:34	Thornaby East Jct	16:46 - 17:03	Eaglescliffe	17:11
Northallerton	17:39	Thirsk	17:46	York	18:23
Colton Jct	18:31	Church Fenton	18:36	Ferrybridge N. Jct	18:47
Moorthorpe	19:15	Rotherham Mas. Jct	19:39	Treeton Jct	19:50
Barrow Hill N. Jct	20:05	Tapton Jct	20:10	Chesterfield	20:11
Clay Cros N. Jct	20:16	Blackwell South Jct	20:27 - 20:36	Alfreton	20:39
Langley Mill	20:47	Toton Centre	20:59	Trent East Jct	21:10
Stenson Jct	21:41	Burton on Trent	22:02 - 22:12	Wichnor Jct	22:23
Lichfield Trent Valley	22:46	Stafford	23:09	Crewe Bas. Hall Jct	23:35
Crewe Basford Hall	23:40 - 23:53	Crewe Coal Yard	00:06	Winsford	00:17
Acton bridge	00:23	Runcorn	00:32	**Ditton**	**00:48**

(Top right) : DRS No.57009 passes Stocksfield on the Tyne Valley Line with 4E38, 02.32 Ditton - Tees Dock on Saturday, 28th July.

The train is easily identifiable, not only by the DRS traction but, by the yellow 'P & O Ferrymasters' containers.

(Centre) : This British weather has a lot to answer for - this is the photographer's first shot in three weeks to the day!

In glorious sunshine, No.57004 passes Ouston, just south of Tyne Yard, on Saturday, 21st July, with 4E38 02.32 Ditton - Tees Dock Intermodal.

As with the previous image, the train has been routed via WCML, Tyne Valley and ECML.

Note the 'Angel of the North' standing proudly on the hillside in the distance.   **Martin Cook (2)**

(Below) : On many occasions this service attracts 2 x Class 57s, like here when Nos.57002 + 57004 pass Burton Salmon with 4M51, 16:10 Tees Dock - Ditton intermodal. The train is on the "Up Pontefract' line, the nearside lines run to Castleford.   **Ian Ball**

Dungeness 'PFAs'

In May, 2-axle 'PFAs' start to appear on the Dungeness flask service (usually 'FNAs') which house brown coloured containers, holding low level waste.

These 'PFAs' are normally seen on the Sellafield - Drigg 'trip', 7C20 / 7C21.

(Top left) : DRS Class 20/3 No.20304 (unbranded) + No.20303 (DRS-branded) make their way through Shortlands on 23rd May with 6M95, the 16:35 Dungeness - Willesden, hauling four 'PFAs'.

(Centre) : Close up view 'PFA' 2-axle flat No.DRSL 92717. These wagons are in the number range DRSL 92703 - BFL 92856.

Richard A. Jones (2)

(Below) : The two Class 20s on 6M95 are seen again, this time crossing Eynsford viaduct as an unidentified Class 319 EMU heads in the opposite direction towards Shoreham.

Alan Hazelden

Dounreay Flasks

DRS start running flask services between Sellafield and Georgemas Junction, running to a new railhead to support the closure of the redundant nuclear site at Dounreay. The facility at Georgemas Junction on the far north rail line will enable fuel to be returned to national stocks where it can be used to generate electricity. The service is:

6M98, 14:45 Georgemas Junction - Carlisle   **2 x DRS 37s** (T 'n' T)

The flasks then go forward on 6C22, Carlisle Kingmoor - Sellafield.

Dounreay nuclear power station was established in 1955, located about 9 miles west of Thurso in Caithness. The remote site was chosen for safety reasons (in case of an explosion!) and the first reactor was surrounded by a 139-foot steel sphere.

The site had three main reactors:

1) **(DMTR)** : The first Dounreay reactors to achieve criticality was the Dounreay Materials Test Reactor (DMTR) in May 1958. This reactor was used to test the performance of materials under intense neutron irradiation. The DMTR closed in 1969.

2) **(DFR)** : The second operational reactor was the Dounreay Fast Reactor (DFR), which achieved criticality on 14 November 1959, but taken offline for decommissioning in 1977.

3) **(PFR)** : The third and final reactor built was the Prototype Fast Reactor (PFR), which achieved criticality in 1974. The reactor was taken offline in 1994, marking the end of nuclear power generation at the site. PFR was a pool-type fast breeder reactor, cooled by liquid sodium and fueled with MOX (Mixed Oxide Fuel). A remotely operated robot dubbed 'The Reactorsaurus' is used to remove waste and contaminated equipment from this reactor as it is too dangerous a task for a human.

44 tonnes of material needs to be removed and decommissioning is required to be complete for a site closure by 2022 - 2025.

DRS Class 37/6s No.37602 and No.37605 (above) top 'n' tail 6M98, 14:45 Georgemas Junction - Carlisle Kingmoor test run for the Dounreay flasks, comprising a single 'FNA' wagon housing a flask. The train is approaching Moy on 5th July 2012, 15 miles south of Inverness on the Highland Line.   **Dave Purser**

Earlseat Blending Coal

Where? The Fife region of Scotland is synonymous with coal, where there have been many opencast sites (Westfields, for example) in the area. Well, another loading point has started to be served by rail and this is at Earl's Seat (see map) on the former Methil branch (off the Edinburgh - Dundee line), which last saw railfreight around the end of the 20th century (1999 / 2000) with carbon dioxide to Cameron Bridge and coal to Methil power station.

The Service :

| 6G26, (WO) 16:52 Earl's Seat - Hunterston | DBS Class 66 |

The coal is being moved to Hunterston, where it will be blended with imported coal and despatched for power station consumption. The first loaded train leaves on 22nd August.

The Rolling Stock : A rake of ex-Milford based 2-axle wagons used on the gypsum and coal diagrams out of Drax. The initial consist is:

MEAs :

391280	391679	391582	391130	391356	391389	391116	391151	391635	391237	391689
391281	391202	391460	391413	391358	391361	391289	391457	391273	391036	391649
391640	391443	391491	391478	391336	391585	391526	391250	391665	391419	391673
391551	391155	391122	391560	391206	391602	391645	391674	391563	391397	391107
391215	391603									

The Route & Timings :

Earlseat	**16:52**	Thornton North Jct	17:02	Glenrothes	17:06
Cowdenbeath	17:26	Dunfermline	17:35	Charlestown Jct	17:36
Longannet	18:08 - 18:18	Alloa Loop	18:34 - 18:46	Alloa	18:48
Cambus	18:50	Causeway Jct	18:54	Stirling	18:57 - 19:01
Larbert	19:12 - 19:22	Larbert Jct	19:25	Carmuirs West Jct	19:26
Greenhill Lower Jct	19:30	Cumbernauld	19:44	Garnqueen North Jct	19:50
Gartsherrie South Jct	19:52	Coatbridge Central	19:53	Langloan Jct	19:55
Carmyle	20:04	Rutherglen East Jct	20:09	Larkfield Jct	20:16
Terminus Jct	20:21	Shields Jct	20:25	Arkleston Jct	20:33 - 20:41
Paisley	20:46	Elderslie	20:49	Dalry	21:07
Kilwinning	21:13	Saltcoats	21:18	Hunterston Jct	21:33
Hunterston	**21:36**				

DBS Class 66/0 No.**66138** has the honour of working the first loaded coal train from Earlseat on 22nd August and the empties are seen being hauled by No.66138 (above) through Glenrothes with Thornton station (in the village of Thornton and at least two miles away from Glenrothes) with 6G25, the 05.06 Falkland Yard - Earlseat consisting of 46 x 'MEAs' for loading. The 'MEAs' arrived at Falkland Yard on a 6S97 service from Milford, hauled by No.66138.   **David Hamilton**

(Bottom left) : A somewhat rare sight, a loaded coal train heading away from Longannet power station - in this case, No.66138 heading the first loaded coal train (6G26) from Earlseat along the 'SAK' by the side of the Firth of Forth, photographed from the Kincardine on Forth Bridge.   **Alastair Blackwood**

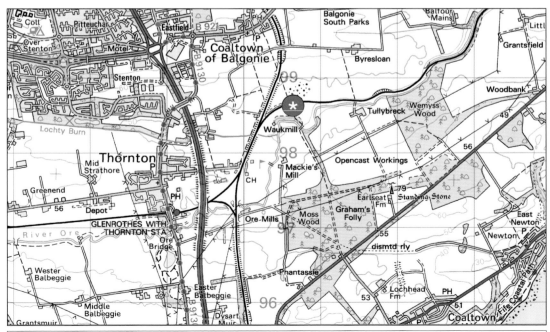

Landranger No.59 St. Andrews - Courtesy Ordnance Survey mapping @ Crown Copyright Media 035/12

6Z36

(Top Left) : On 30th March, FHH No.66622 is allocated to work 6Z36, the 13:00 Blackburn Gilbraiths - Barrow Hill, and is seen running into Horbury Cutting where the floodlights of the now closed Healey Mills yard can be made out in the background.

These 'HIA' wagons are seen quite often on the Calder Valley line, usually heading empty from the Aire Valley to Guide Bridge sidings, but rarely loaded.

Derek Holmes

6M22

(Centre) : An occasional DBS train runs from Moreton on Lugg to Leeds Hunslet and the empty hoppers return to Peak Forest via the Calder Valley main line and Standedge.

Here are the empties off one of these occasional trains, where the use of orange ex-RMC 'JGAs' and a DBS-livery 'shed' certainly spices things up. On 30th May, No.66101 is passing Mirfield, running as 6M22, 12:20 Leeds Hunslet - Peak Forest, which is the same code as the Hunslet cement empties! **Derek Holmes**

6E08

(Bottom Left) : On 12th July No.66616 is about to cross Thrumpton level crossing at Retford with 6E08, Earles Sidings - West Burton flyash empties.

The line is the former MS & LR (Manchester, Sheffield and Lincolnshire Railway) formed by amalgamation in 1847, changing its name to the Great Central Railway in 1897 in anticipation of the opening in 1899 of its London Extension. **Mick Tindall**

Construction Commodities

Gritstone

Following a previous DBS-operated trial from Blackburn to Radlett (6Z33), FHH operate a new trial in March, moving gritstone to Kennett (between Ely and Bury St Edmunds), loaded to 20 'HIAs'.

This particular working also brings the unusual sight of 'HIAs' on the Copy Pit route between Blackburn and Hebden Bridge. The working is split in to two separate legs:

6Z36, 13:00 Blackburn - Barrow Hill   6Z37, 08:03 Barrow Hill - Kennett

Gritstone or Grit is a hard, coarse-grained, siliceous sandstone, quarried for building material, especially from the gritstone edges of the Pennines and Peak District. It is formed from sediments laid down in the late (upper) Paleozoic era, in the Carboniferous period.

Flyash

Also known as Pulverised Fuel Ash (PFA), Flyash is a by-product from coal-fired power stations and is supplied to the ready-mixed concrete and concrete products markets as a cement replacement. Cement is a heavy contributor to CO_2 emissions, so the less used in concrete manufacture, the lower the impact on the environment - flyash, therefore, reduces the *'Carbon Footprint'*. Flyash is conveyed to Earles (Hope) in 'PCA' 2-axle cement wagons, the same type used on the Earles to Dewsbury and West Thurrock cement flows. The respective flyash flows to Earles are:

6M45, 15:00 Drax - Earles sidings

6Z08, 13:40 West Burton - Earles

Bagged Cement :

Powdered cement in bags is now being transported from Oxwellmains to Aberdeen in bogie 'Ferrywaggons' in addition to the usual 2-axle 'PCA' tanks. The reporting details of this flow are given below, but it is the returning empties which provide the best photographic opportunities.

6A65, (MWO) 06:13 Oxwellmains - Aberdeen Craiginches

In glorious sunshine, two 'Ferrywaggons' can be seen directly behind FHH Class No.66610 (above) as it passes Elliot, near Arbroath, on 23rd May with 6B32, 16:52 (MWO) Craiginches - Oxwellmains empty cement. The coastline between Arbroath and Dundee is blessed with some of the best 'Links' golf courses in the world, the most famous at Carnoustie, which can host a British Open Championship.   **Jim** Ramsay

Wool Sand

6M42, (MX) 15:00 Wool - Neasden (loaded)
6O49, (FX) 10:51 Neasden - Wool

This is a particularly interesting flow.

Firstly, the empties (6O49) can only be loaded at Wool by first running further west to Dorchester South station.

Secondly, this is the *only* scheduled freight service Dorchester ever sees. It works like this ....

The empties from Neasden arrive at Dorchester South then reverse into the sidings adjacent to the signal box, where the wagons are split into two portions.

One portion is left in the 'Down' siding. The other is drawn forward into the station, the loco runs round and departs for Wool with portion 1. After shunting the wagons into the MOD sidings at Wool, the loco returns to Dorchester for portion 2.

The empties cannot go directly into Wool as there is no crossover from the 'Down Main', although this may be rectified when the main line between Bournemouth and Weymouth is re-signalled.

(Top Left) : On 26th June, FHH No.66523 has just dropped 1/2 the wagons off at Dorchester South and is in the process of running round portion 1.

(Centre) : No.66523 explodes into action as it departs with portion 1, portion 2 can be seen in the siding.

(Below) : Seven days earlier, No.66530 is seen arriving at Dorchester with 6O49, Neasden - Wool sand empties, formed of 'JRAs'. **Mike Hemming (3)**

Holybourne - Harwich

Hot on the Greenergy deal (see overleaf), GBRf secure another petroleum-related flow, this time taking crude oil from Holybourne to the Carless refinery at Harwich. Whilst details seem a little sketchy, it appears that this flow supplements the condensate (light crude oil) derived from southern North Sea gas production through the Bacton terminal, North Walsham. If the heavier crude oil from Holybourne is a replacement feedstock, the flow operates rather sporadically, to say the least, a bit like the old Aberdeen - Harwich (6S60 / 6L59) 'Mud oil' service !

> 6L34, 20:03 (FO) Holybourne - Harwich   **GBRf Class 66**

The train comprises 10 VTG (**V**ereinigte **T**anklager und Transportmittel **G**mbH) 'TEAs' ....

80163	87171	87575	87579	87576	87485	87669	87572	80167	87166

.... and provides one of the most interesting routes for this type of train, especially with GBRf traction - bogie tanks running from the old Southern Region, across London, to East Anglia.

(Above) : In this view, No.66703 'Doncaster PSB 1981 - 2002' approaches Woking on 20th July with 6L34, Holybourne - Harwich loaded crude oil tanks, half-an-hour into the 125 mile journey. Upon arriving at Parkeston, nearly one hour is spent negotiating entry into the Carless refinery with reversals at Harwich 'Up TIP Sidings', Headshunt and Carless Refinery Headshunt!   **Simon Howard**

The Route :
Holybourne (dep) 20:03

Aldershot (20:19)	Aldershot North Jct (20:24)	Ash Vale (20:26)
Pirbright Jct (20:31)	Woking (20:37)	Byfleet & New Haw (20:44)
Addlestone Jct (20:46)	Virginia Water (20:54)	Staines (21:12)
Hounslow (21:23)	Brentford (21:27)	Kew East Jct (21:32 to 22:18)
South Acton Jct (22:23)	Acton Wells Jct (22:27)	Willesden Jct. High Level (22:31)
Gospel Oak (22:40)	Camden Road (22:54)	Canonbury (22:59)
Lea Jct (23:12)	Stratford (23:22)	Stratford Signal L295 (23:23 to 23:40)
Chelmsford (00:11)	Colchester (00:38)	Manningtree (00:47)
Parkeston (01:00 - 01:12)	Harwich (01:15 to 01:20)	Parkeston (01:25 to 01:45)

Harwich Refinery (arr) 01:51

GBRf Secure Greenergy Deal

GBRf secure a major new contract with petroleum supplier Greenergy, the UK's leading supplier of petrol, biofuel and diesel, to haul petroleum products from Immingham to the newly refurbished Inver Terminal at Queen Alexandra Dock, Cardiff.

Greenergy supply about a fifth of the UK's road fuel, making 120,000 truck deliveries per year to supermarkets, oil companies and forecourts. GBRf are helping to reduce the carbon footprint by moving bulk loads by rail, assisting the truck fleet in its deliveries.

GBRf will initially operate this flow twice a week, with a view to extending the service to other terminals across the UK. However, from an enthusiast's perspective, as the loaded train runs overnight, photographic opportunities are restricted to the return empties.

6V11, 22:14 Lindsey - Cardiff Docks   **GBRf Class 66**

The first train runs on 15th December 2011, hauled by No.66717, consisting of 16 'TDAs':

86939	86943	86938	86954	86956	86937	86948	86955
86959	86944	86958	86953	86952	86947	86960	86962

On 29th May, GBRf Class 66/7 No.66715 'Valour....' (top) passes Bullo Pill, near Newnham, Gloucestershire, with 6E01, 17:17 Cardiff Docks - Peterborough empty petroleum tanks. After staging at Peterborough, the 'TDAs' will go forward as 6E87, Peterborough - Lindsey.

A month earlier, 24th April, No.66729 'Derby County' (above) is captured in this atmospheric composition at Severn Tunnel Junction crossing from the 'Up Relief' onto the 'Up Main' with the empty tanks - also, 6E01, 17:17 Cardiff Docks - Peterborough.   **Peter Slater (2)**

Euro Porte's Class 92 No.92032 'IMechE Railway Division' (above) hauls brand new bogie petroleum tanks through Shoreham (Kent) on Thursday, 23rd August having come through the Channel Tunnel and now running as 6M92, Dollands Moor - Willesden. These tanks (see overleaf for more details) are to be used by 'Greenergy', who have taken over the operations of 'Petroplus' who went into administration recently, and will see use on the Lindsey - Cardiff Docks flow.   **Edward Clarkson**

Having arrived at Willesden, the Class 92 hands over to a GBRf Class 66/7 for the remainder of the new tank's journey to Humberside. No.66729 'Derby County' (below) is seen passing New Zealand Bridge, Sandy, with the 'Greenergy' bogie, now running as 6E92, 13:12 Willesden - Lindsey.   **Nigel Gibbs**

Wagons Roll

A sign of a buoyant railfreight market is the arrival of new wagons. During July and August, new rolling stock arrives in the UK, which will see use on Colas Rail and GBRf contracts.

GBRf : Petroleum Products Bogie Tanks

Carkind : TEA **Design Code : TE048B** **Pool :** **111**

70.7792.001-0	70.7792.002-8	70.7792.003-6	70.7792.004-4	70.7792.005-1
70.7792.006-9	70.7792.007-7	70.7792.008-5	70.7792.009-3	70.7792.010-1
70.7792.011-9	70.7792.012-7	70.7792.013-5	70.7792.014-3	70.7792.015-0
70.7792.016-8	70.7792.017-6	70.7792.018-4	70.7792.019-2	70.7792.020-0
70.7792.021-8	70.7792.022-6	70.7792.023-4	70.7792.024-2	70.7792.025-9

Carkind : TEA **Design Code : TE048A** **Pool :** **728**

70.7792.026-7	70.7792.027-5	70.7792.028-3	70.7792.029-1	70.7792.030-9
70.7792.031-7	70.7792.032-5	70.7792.033-3	70.7792.034-1	70.7792.035-8
70.7792.036-6	70.7792.037-4	70.7792.038-2	70.7792.039-0	70.7792.040-8
70.7792.041-6	70.7792.042-4	70.7792.043-2	70.7792.044-0	70.7792.045-7
70.7792.046-5	70.7792.047-3	70.7792.048-1	70.7792.049-9	70.7792.050-7

The wagons come in two distinct liveries:
- blue with 'Greenergy' branding in white lettering
- lime green with 'Efficient' branding in white lettering.

(Above) : Close up view of the new Greenergy 'TEA' petroleum bogie tanks - the green liveried tanks branded 'Efficient' and the blue ones branded 'Greenergy'. The wagons are in the consist of 6M92, Dollands Moor - Wembley, passing through Shoreham. **Edward Clarkson**

(Top Right) : Ex-Freightliner No.66740 (still in green livery) makes a fine sight as it passes the signal box at Blaydon on 3rd September with a rake of six, nicely cleaned up, PolyBulk covered hoppers (Covhops) in tow. The train is 6Z58, 11:00 Hardendale - Lackenby.

Apparently, previous efforts to run this train have always been cancelled, due to operating problems at Hardendale for non-DBS services involving the operation of the level crossing lights. It would seem this problem has been resolved.

GBRf : Lime Polybulks		Carkind : JIA		
70.9382.000-5	70.9382.003-9	70.9382.005-4	70.9382.006-2	70.9382.007-0
70.9382.008-8	70.9382.009-6	70.9382.012-0	70.9382.013-8	70.9382.014-6
70.9382.015-3	70.9382.017-9	70.9382.026-0	70.9382.027-8	70.9382.028-6
70.9382.029-4	70.9382.030-2	70.9382.034-4	70.9382.040-1	70.9382.041-9
70.9382.044-3	70.9382.046-8	70.9382.047-6	70.9382.048-4	70.9382.049-2
70.9382.051-8	70.9382.052-6			

(Above) : GBRF No.66703 'Doncaster PSB 1981 - 2002', still sporting original 'Bluebird' livery, passes Broomhaugh (near Riding Mill) on the Tyne Valley Line with 6Z58, the 11:00 Hardendale - Lackenby limestone 'Polybulks' on a sunny Wednesday, 22nd August. The term 'PolyBulk' refers to a wagon which can carry many types of bulk commodity, such as grain, lime and sand. **Martin Cook (2)**

(Left) : Close up of reworked Cargowaggon No.84.3523.048-0, at Shoreham on 31st August in the consist of 6Z47, Dollands Moor - Gloucester. These wagons will be used to convey timber from Baglan Bay, Carlisle, Teigngrace and any other loading points.　**Ian Cuthbertson**

(Below) : Colas Rail 47 No.47739 'Robin of Templecombe' is captured hauling the converted timber carriers (6Z47) through Sonning Cutting, Reading, bound for Gloucester.　**Simon Howard**

Colas : Timber Carriers

Carkind : IWA　　　Design Code : IWE963B　　Pool :　Various

84.3523.011-8	84.3523.017-5	84.3523.019-1	84.3523.022-5	84.3523.023-3
84.3523.025-8	84.3523.026-6	84.3523.027-4	84.3523.028-2	84.3523.029-0
84.3523.030-8	84.3523.031-6	84.3523.032-4	84.3523.033-2	84.3523.034-0
84.3523.035-7	84.3523.036-5	84.3523.037-3	84.3523.038-1	84.3523.039-9
84.3523.040-7	84.3523.041-5	84.3523.042-3	84.3523.043-1	84.3523.044-9
84.3523.045-6	84.3523.046-4	84.3523.047-2	84.3523.048-0	84.3523.049-8

Dutch registered wagons.

Converted from 'IWA' 'Cargowaggons' (83.80.4741.000-9 to 099-1).

Originally built between 1987 - 1988 by Waggon Union.

More Class 60s in Traffic

DBS start 2012 with more Class 60s in traffic than in previous years - **11** to be exact - compared to only **6** on the corresponding day in 2011 and **5** in 2010, which is great news for enthusiasts.

This is the state of play on Monday, 2nd January:

Loco	Pool	Location	Allocated WTT
60007	WCBK	Tunstead	6F05, Tunstead - Oakleigh
60011	WCAI	Warrington	
60024	WCAK	Tunstead	
60039	WCAI	Fiddlers Ferry	6F07, Fiddlers Ferry - Liverpool BKTM
60045	WCAI	Warrington	
60054	WCBI	Margam	
60071	WCBI	Margam	6B07, Margam - Robeston
60074	WFMU	Toton	6K50, Toton - Crewe Basford Hall
60091	WCBI	Jarrow	6D43, Jarrow - Lindsey
60096	WCBI	Warrington	6F78, Fiddlers Ferry - Liverpool BKTM
60099	WCAI	Toton	

With so many more Class 60s coming on stream following overhaul, this extensive feature follows the Class 60s in traffic during the first six months of 2012.

60011 : What a wonderful sight .... after being ousted on the iron ore circuit over two years ago by the DBS Class 66s, Class 60s are still occasional and welcome performers on such trains. On 3rd February, No.60011 (above) leads 6T26, 14:45 Immingham Bulk Terminal - Santon loaded iron ore for Scunthorpe steel works and is seen passing Ulceby. The 'tug' looks perfectly at home atop the bauxite-stained 'JTA' and 'JUA' hoppers. **Nathan Seddon**

Overhaul Schedule

More Class 60s will be repaired throughout 2012, but not all as part of the Class 60 'Super Tug' overhaul programme. This will release more Class 66s to work on the seasonal RHTT 'leaf-busting' trains in the autumn, leaving the Class 60s to work more front-line freight duties. These are the '60s' (as identified on 24th February) scheduled for overhaul / repair in 2012:

Loco	Repair Work	Expected	Current Restrictions	
60003	Crankcase + Block	September	(HD) Hauled 'Dead'	
			(NJ) One Journey to Depot Only	
60012	Crankcase + Block	June	(QX) Quarantined (Out of use)	
60015	General Overhaul	April		
60017	General Overhaul	July	(NJ) One Journey to Depot Only	
			(HD) Hauled 'Dead'	
			(QX) Quarantined (Out of use)	
60021	Bogie Change	September		
60033	Main Generator / Alternator	June	(HD) Hauled 'Dead'	
			(NJ) One Journey to Depot Only	
60040	General Overhaul	May	(NJ) One Journey to Depot Only	
			(LE) Light Loco / DIT for Repairs	
60059	General Overhaul	March	(WD) Wheelset Dispensation	
			(HD) Hauled 'Dead'	
60063	Paint / Respray	March	(TR) Test Run	
60077	Crankcase + Block	?	(HD) Hauled 'Dead'	
			(NJ) One Journey to Depot Only	
60080	Engine Repairs	September		
60085	Bogie Change	September		
60088	Bogie Change	September		
60092	'On Decision'	December		

60063 (above) is seen on the seldom photographed North Stafford Junction - Uttoxeter - Stoke on Trent line approaching Uttoxeter on 29th March. The train is 6Z15, Burton Wetmore Sidings - Warrington Arpley and a consist of overhauled china clay slurry tanks.   **Mick Tindall**

Test Runs....

60079 : This is the first 'tug' to be refurbished in 2012, released to traffic on 2nd February, and is booked for a test run to Peterborough.

Looking resplendent in DBS red, No.60079 (top right) prepares to leave Toton with 6Z60, the 11:30 Toton - Peterborough, formed of 15 'Autoballasters'. **Craig Adamson**

Meanwhile, No.60079 (centre) is now nearing journey's end, rumbling through Bainton on the Stamford - Peterborough line with 6Z60.

No.60079 later returns to Toton, running as 6Z79, the 14:10hrs ex-Peterborough. **James Welham**

60074 *'Teenage Spirit'* : Just a few weeks after overhaul and repainting into Teenage Cancer Trust livery, No.60074 'Teenage Spirit' (below) heads south through Sherburn in Elmet on 12th January with 6Z53, the 1350 York Engineers Yard - Scunthorpe rail delivery train, following repair. The set will then be reloaded with rail from the TATA steel plant.

Nathan Seddon

Coal

Liverpool BKTM - Fiddlers Ferry

The use of 'buffer-fitted' HTA bogie coal hoppers has enabled Class 60s to remain working on the power station circuit, mainly out of Liverpool Bulk Import Terminal to Fiddlers Ferry power station on Merseyside.

There can, theoretically, be up to 7 rakes of 'HTAs' utilising the buffer-fitted vehicles, which are numbered:

330191	330215	330331	330332	330374	330381	330472
330493	330503	330564	330714	330734	330745	331083

By way of example, typically, there are three Class 60 diagrams workings out of Liverpool Bulk Import Terminal:

Diagram 1:
6F89, 06:12 Liverpool BKTM - Fiddlers Ferry
6F84, 16:56 Liverpool - Fiddlers Ferry

Diagram 2:
6F81, 09:14 Liverpool - Fiddlers Ferry
6F85, 20:06 Liverpool - Fiddlers Ferry

Diagram 3:
6F74, 12:11 Liverpool - Fiddlers Ferry
6F77, 21:22 Liverpool - Fiddlers Ferry

(Right) : Buffer-fitted 'HTA' No.330332 at Walton Old Junction, Warrington. Martin Buck

60011 : (Bottom Left)
Framed by the signal, No.60011 nudges forward on to the headshunt at Latchford, Warrington, with train 6F81, the 09:14 Liverpool BKTM - Fiddlers Ferry loaded coal. The train has just crossed the River Mersey and waits the 'RA' to proceed to the run-round sidings (see top right). **David Hayes**

60045 : (Top Right)
'The Permanent Way institution' :
Still sporting original EWS colours and nameplates, No.60045 crawls to a halt at Latchford Sidings on 16th January, prior to running-round with 6F74, the 12:11 Liverpool BKTM - Fiddlers Ferry.

60099 : (Bottom Right)
This delightful composition shows 'Tata Steel' liveried No.60099 passing Sankey Bridges in the western outskirts of Warrington on 16th January with 6F78, the 11:30 Fiddlers Ferry - Liverpool BKTM coal empties, having worked 6F89 earlier in the day. The 'tug' will return on the loaded 6F84, 16:56 Liverpool BKTM - Fiddlers Ferry. **Neil Harvey (2)**

6F74 ▲ **▼ 6F78**

The Old EWS Guise

60065 *'Spirit of JAGUAR'* (top left) passes Acton Bridge on the WCML and is heading south with a 6L50, Carnforth - Crewe Basford Hall engineer's train, formed mainly of Network Rail 'JNA' (Falcon) bogie ballast wagons. **Ian Ball**

60039 (centre) is stabled at Eastleigh 'Virtual Quarry' during the evening of 13th March waiting to leave with loaded ballast for an overnight engineer's possession.

Ballast is principally received from the Mendip quarries and is stockpiled at Eastleigh VQ pending distribution. As can be seen, ballast is loaded/unloaded using mechanical grabs. **Simon Howard**

60024 (below) is looking extremely tatty and in need of a fresh coat of paint, as it passes Plumley on 8th February with 6H03, 10:47 Oakleigh - Tunstead empty hoppers.

This is a daily booked Class 60 turn working out the Peak Forest. The rake of Brunner Mond 'JEAs' tail all the way back to Plumley signal box. **Nathan Seddon**

'Tugs' To The Rescue

60063 (above) makes a rare appearance on 6V67, 03:53 (FX) Redcar - Margam loaded coke, albeit due to the failure of No.66086, which expired on 4th April near Broadholme, Derby. No.60063 is sent to rescue the dead 'shed' and 'HTAs' and the eye-catching consist is photographed passing Duffryn, near Newport.

60079 (below) is sent (0Z99, Llanwern - Gloucester) to rescue failed No.60007 'The Spirit of John Kendell' on 6B13, Robeston - Westerleigh loaded Murco bogie tanks. The 'tug' had been experiencing power problems since Pontyclun and eventually fails with a loss of power at Gloucester. The double-headed '60s' pass Charfield, running about 213 minutes late.   **Jamie Squibbs (2)**

Fuel Oil

6D70 : Many depots around the country receive fuel for their loco fleets by rail, transported in either 'TDA' / 'TEA' bogie tanks or 2-axle 'TTA' tank wagons. In this superb atmospheric composition, No.60079 (above) runs alongside the banks of the Stainforth & Keadby Canal at Crowle on 6th March with 6D70, 14:20 (WO) Neville Hill - Lindsey fuel oil empties, formed of five bogie tanks. **Alan Padley**

6E38 : No.60091 (below) makes another appearance on 6E38, 13:54 Colnbrook - Lindsey empty bogie tanks on 8th March and is seen approaching Leagrave and in better light than the watery sun on this stretch of the Midland Main Line two days previously. This particular flow is aviation fuel for Heathrow Airport. Due to operational constraints, the loaded train (6V70) is staged en-route at Didcot Yard. **Nigel Gibbs**

Trans-Pennine Tanks

6E32 : No.60091 (above) comes off the 'Copy Pit' line from Blackburn at Hall Royd Junction to join the Calder Valley main line (via Hebden Bridge) on 20th April with 6E32, 08:55 (MWFO) Preston Docks - Lindsey empty bitumen bogie tanks. These VTG tanks were introduced in November 2010 ('ICA' carkind / 'Zaefns' UIC code) to replace 'life expired' CAIB and VTG bogie tanks built in 1986/1987 by C C Crump.

6M22 : Tunstead supplies cement to Leeds Hunslet (6E28), Walsall (6M09) and Willesden (6A50) using bogie cement tank wagons, a hopper-based design, but with a 'JGA' TOPS code! In a brief spell of sunshine, No.60054 (below) climbs through Paddock Cutting, Huddersfield, on 9th March with 6M22, 12:20 Hunslet - Tunstead empties. It looks like the trees will soon encroach and spoil the view - pity!   **Neil Harvey (2)**

60074

Just out of the box! Looking great after a fresh coat of paint, No.60074 'Teenage Cancer Trust' (above) passes Knabble Bridge (near Barnetby) running over 200 minutes late on 14th January, with 6E46, 04:35 Kingsbury - Lindsey empty petroleum tanks. Twelve months ago, No.60073 passed the same spot on 6E46 (Loco Review 2012, Page 9) trudging through several inches of snow!   **Richard Armstrong**

With dark clouds looming, in a lucky burst of sunshine, No.60074 (below) shunts the loaded tanks back into Jarrow Oil Terminal on Monday, 13th February, having arrived with 6N03, the 01:13 Lindsey - Jarrow. No.60074 was named 'Teenager Cancer Trust' on 1st March 2008 and, along with No.60099, is the only 'tug' to sport a 3rd party colour scheme.   **Martin Cook**

A 'tug swap' takes place on 25th February and No.60074 (top right) returns to South Wales, working 6V40, 04:25 Scunthorpe - Cardiff Tidal steel empties, which is seen passing Woolaston, near Lydney.

The 'tug' comes off at Newport ADJ and goes forward on 6B04 to Margam (see centre image).

Oh, the ignominy of it, No.60074 being tucked in behind a 'shed' ....

Later, on 25th February, DBS Class 66/0 No.66006 (centre) passes Coedkernow, west of Newport, with 6B04, the 14:48 Llanwern - Margam steel empties.

Shades of Blue .... on 27th March, No.60074 (below) is approaching Pilning with 6B33, 13:35 Theale-Robeston empty petroleum tanks, just as an unidentified HST heads in the opposite direction, presumed to be 1L74, the 15:55 Cardiff Central - London Paddington. From Pilning, the line descends for three miles at a gradient of 1 in 100 into Severn Tunnel, which is 4 miles 624 yards long, although only $2\frac{1}{4}$ miles of tunnel are under the river.

Peter Slater (3)

6H27

The Hindlow 'Trip'

6H22, 11:08 Tunstead - Hindlow   **6H23, 14:16 Hindlow - Tunstead**

In January 1988, limestone for the lime plant at Hindlow was transferred to Tunstead, which is on the former main line from Manchester to Derby, following the end of quarrying at Hindlow. Lime is 'tripped' to Peak Forest, thence on a 6F65 wagonload service to Warrington.

Tunstead quarry is now operated by Tarmac and was once part of the ICI conglomerate, until de-merger in the early 1990's. Whilst there are many aggregate flows originating in the Peak Forest area which attract Class 60 haulage, the Hindlow 'trip' is of particular interest. It is operationally complex, involving run-rounds, despite a journey distance of under 10 miles!

The loaded train service (6H22 weekdays / **6H27 Sunday**) operates as follows:

Tunstead Sidings - Great Rocks ('Down & Up' Through Siding)	1 mile
Great Rocks - Buxton 'Up Relief' Sidings	1.5 miles
Buxton - Hindlow (Briggs Sidings)	4.5 miles

(The return empties run in the reverse order.)

Out & about with No.60011 on Sunday, 15th April, working the Hindlow 'trip'......

Note, on Sunday, the reporting code changes to 6H27 and 6H29, respectively.

60011

The first image shows No.60011 (above) heading past Tunstead along the single 'Down and Up Goods' line on its way to Buxton and a second reversal with 6H27, 11:08 Tunstead - Hindlow loaded limestone, having already affected a reversal at Great Rocks.

At Buxton, No.60011 (top left) sits in the 'Up Relief' sidings awaiting clearance to proceed. The sidings are adjacent to the main passenger line which links Buxton with Stockport and Manchester Piccadilly.

Finally, a delightful rural setting on the Hindlow branch, once the Buxton and High Peak Junction line. No.60011 (bottom left) passes Staden (*aka* Harpur Hill) with 6H27, making slow progress towards its destination. The consist of the train on this particular occasion is a mix of 'JGA' bogie hoppers - the distinctive orange liveried ex-RMC hoppers built in 1986 and much newer ones built by VTG.   **Ian Ball (3)**

On 11th March, No.60091 (top left) powers past Crabley Creek with a slightly early running 6T62, 14:50 Brough - Doncaster Up Decoy Yard engineer's train, consisting mainly of 'MRA' bogie side tipping ballast wagons, 'YWA' 'Salmon' track panel carriers and some 'OBA' 2-axle wagons.

Crabley Creek is situated two miles west of Brough on the Hull line, which is still controlled by semaphore signals between Ferriby and Gilberdyke. **James Skoyles**

On 17th February, No.60091 (centre) is seen on less strenuous duties shunting a single 'BLA' bogie steel coil wagon, whilst acting as a 'super 60' super shunter at Margam Knuckle Yard. **Mark Thomas**

On 14th June, the usual DBS 'shed' rostered for 6O15, 17:30 Mossend - Eastleigh wagonload service turns up with a Class 60 instead.

No.60091 (below) is seen running alongside the embankment carrying Battledown Flyover, Basingstoke, with 10 empty 'TTA' fuel oil tanks in the consist. **Simon Howard**

.... The Return To traffic

No.60040 returns to traffic in June embellished in DBS colours, but still retaining the commemorative nameplate 'The Territorial Army Centenary'. On 27th July, No.60040 (above) rounds the curve at the site of Portskewett station with 6V05, 10:01 Round Oak - Margam empty steel, as ATW Class 150 'Sprinter' No.150 257 enters the scene with 2G58, 12:12 Cardiff Central - Cheltenham Spa. **Chris Perkins**

60040

Toton Primes .... No.60040 for its re-paint - unfortunately, not in the all-over maroon livery, which was applied in June 2008 to mark the Territorial Army's Centenary. This is the last time we will see No.60040 (inset) in maroon livery as it stands in Toton yard on 27th May. **Craig Adamson**

No.60015 (above) is seen fresh off overhaul, passing Souldrop on 24th May with 6F93, 11:03 St Pancras - Ketton cement empties, formed of the distinctive 'Castle Cement' branded 2-axle 'PCA' tanks. **Nigel Gibbs**

60015

Rare traction and even rarer wagons for 6E14, 16:10 Seaforth - Tinsley. On 24th May, No.60015 (below) heads down the Calder Valley near Luddenfoot with empty 'BVA' bogie steel flat wagons instead of the usual 'BDA' / 'BEAs'. The 'BVAs' are fitted with 'cassettes' so steel can be quickly loaded / unloaded. Normally, these wagons see use on 'Steelbridge' traffic from Tinsley to Immingham.   **Neil Harvey**

Another rare move takes place during 29th & 30th May when No.60015 is called upon to take a new Javelin EMU to York for the 'Railfest' exhibition. On the 29th, No.60015 (above) is seen passing West Ealing with 6Z60, Eastleigh - Wembley and the barrier wagons for the next day's move. **Ian Cuthbertson**

On the 30th, No.60015 (below) passes Eaton Lane, Retford in charge of 6Z30, the 08:49 Dollands Moor - York, conveying Class 395 No.395019 (inset) in the consist, where the front of the train looks more like a 'Speedlink' freight than brake runners for the Javelin. **Alan Padley (2)**

60011

A rarity at Alton on 15th June ....

No.60011 (top left) is seen approaching Alton on the single line with 6Y32, 08:24 (MWO) Fawley - Holybourne empty bogie tanks, slowing for the stop at Alton where it will reverse. The single line extends from Farnham to Alton.

Having arrived at Alton, No.60011 (left) detaches from the tanks and runs round in the station in order to retrace its steps to Holybourne, where the tanks will be propelled back into the loading terminal.

In the background is Maunsell SR U Class 2-6-0 steam engine No.31806, built at Brighton Works in 1928, and is one of more than 20 steam engines based at the Mid Hants Railway.

This heritage line is also affectionately known as the 'Watercress Line' due to the transportation of watercress from the beds in Alresford to London. This heritage railway was saved by enthusiastic volunteers in 1973 and now runs for 10 miles between the market towns of Alresford and Alton.

Crude Oil

'Holybourne Tanks'

6Y34, 20:03 (MWO) Holybourne - Eastleigh Yard
6B41, 06:56 (MTO) Eastleigh Yard - Fawley
6B93, 09:38 (ThO) Eastleigh Yard - Fawley
6Y32, 08:24 (MWO) Fawley - Holybourne

The oil sidings at Holybourne (2 miles east of Alton) is situated on the Woking - Aldershot - Alton line and despatches crude oil to Fawley refinery twice a week in bogie tank wagons. The crude oil originates from the Humbly Grove oil field and is piped to the terminal.

6Y34 is a normally a solid 'shed' working but, surprisingly, on 15th June, it is worked by No.60011, bringing rare traction to a route starved of such traction. The route is as follows:

Fawley / Redbridge / Southampton / St. Denys	16 miles
St Denys / Fareham / Cosham / Havant	24 miles
Havant / Petersfield / Haslemere / Godalming / Shalford Junction / Guildford	37 miles
Guildford / Ash / Aldershot South Junction / Aldershot North Junction	7 miles
Aldershot North Junction / Aldershot / Farnham / Alton (Run Round) / Holybourne	16 miles
Total Mileage :	100 miles

Fuel Oil

'Colnbrook Tanks'

6V70, 22:05 Lindsey - Colnbrook   **6E38, 13:54 Colnbrook - Lindsey**

The Total / Fina oil terminal at Colnbrook is at the end of a three mile spur off the Great Western Main Line at West Drayton, on what was once the Staines & West Drayton Railway. The terminal receives aviation fuel from Lindsey oil refinery for Heathrow Airport.

In addition, the branch sees aggregate trains to the Bardon terminal at Thorney Hill (FHH), plus stone (DBS) and a departmental service (FHH) to Colnbrook

60007

No.60007 (above) is about half-a-mile away from reaching its destination on a very wet 29th April. It is seen passing Colnbrook Logistics Centre and the Foster Yeoman aggregate discharge sidings with the inbound 6V70 train of loaded tanks which, on this particular day, had started off from Didcot having recessed there overnight. The distinctive yellow and red branding on the Boeing aeroplane nose on the left of view is a dead give away for DHL.   **Simon Howard (3)**

(Overleaf)

60099 : (Page 82) : This super composition shows the village of Lydgate drowsing in the sun on 20th June while No.60099 crosses the viaduct above with 6E32, 08:55 Preston Docks - Lindsey. Lydgate is about mid-way between Cornholme and Todmorden; Coal Clough Wind Farm is visible on the hillside.   **Neil Harvey**

60059 *'Swinden Dalesman'* : (Page 83) : Despite losing its distinctive Loadhaul black & orange livery, at least No.60059 retained its name following overhaul, after which it went immediately to Peak Forest to resume working. On 26th May, the 'tug' is seen crossing Chapel Milton Viaduct with 6H60, 15:22 Hope Street - Peak Forest empty limestone bogie hoppers. No.60059 has come via Chinley and is now traversing the single line which links Chinley North Junction and Chinley South Junction.   **Mick Tindall**

2011 Late Arrivals

70013 - 70016

18th December 2011 : MSV 'BBC Colorado' berths at Newport Docks and unloads:

No.70013 No.70014 No.70015 No.70016

22nd December 2011 : All four locos are allocated to Freightliner's Heavy Haul DFGH pool. Locos moved to Crewe Basford Hall by Class 66/6 No.66622

2nd January 2012 : Allocations:

70013 Basford Hall
70014 Basford Hall
70015 Fiddlers Ferry 4F03, 15:15 Fiddlers Ferry - Ellesmere Port
70016 Midland Road

2012 Arrivals

70017 - 70020

Arrival date	Transporter Ship	Docks	Class 70s
10th January	MSV 'Atlantic Companion'	Seaforth, Liverpool.	No.70017
20th January	MSV 'Atlantic Cartier'	Seaforth.	No.70018
16th February	MSV 'Atlantic Cartier'	Seaforth	No.70019
16th February	MSV 'Atlantic Cartier'	Seaforth	No.70020

The arrival of No.70020 marks the final 'Powerhaul' Class 70 in the Freightliner fleet.

First Moves : 20th January : 70017 4L95, Ditton - Ipswich Yard
14th February : 70018 4L82, Ditton - Felixstowe (to Basford Hall)
27th February : 70019 4L82, Ditton - Felixstowe (to Basford Hall)
28th February : 70020 4K64, Garston - Basford Hall

70013

Semaphores a plenty .... on 5th May, No.70013 (above) starts to pile on the power after being looped at Craven Arms with 4V22, the 09:30 Fiddlers Ferry - Stoke Gifford coal empties. Five separate sets of ex-GWR lower quadrant signals can be seen in this view.

On 24th April, No.70013 (bottom left) approaches Stafford from the south in charge of 6U77, 13:44 (FO) Mountsorrel - Crewe VQ loaded ballast, formed of 'IOA' 'Gondolas'. This flow is booked Class 70 haulage, which runs as 6C64 on Monday / Wednesday to Carlisle VQ. **Mike Hemming (2)**

Fleet Summary

The first time that all 19 members of the 'Powerhaul' Class 70 fleet are available to work is 29th February and here is a summary of their respective positions at 06:30hrs.

Loco	Pool	Location	Allocation	Type of Train
70001	DFGI	Leeds, Midland Road		
70002	DFGH	Garston		
70003	DFGH	Hunslet Yard		
70004	DFGH	Leeds, Midland Road		
70005	DFGH	Crewe, Basford Hall	6C16, Basford Hall - Carlisle Yard	Departmental
70006	DFGH	York, Holgate Sidings	4S75, Drax - Killoch	Coal Empties
70007	DFGI	Lawley Street	4L77, Lawley Street - Felixstowe	Freightliner
70008	DFGI	Trafford Park	4O22, Trafford Park - Southampton	Freightliner
70009	DFGI	Garston	0K42, Garston - Basford Hall	Light Engine
70010	DFGH	Carlisle Yard		
70011	DFGH	Portbury Dock		
70013	DFGH	Fiddlers Ferry		
70014	DFGH	Crewe, Basford Hall	4V04, Basford Hall - Portbury Dock	Coal Empties
70015	DFGH	Leeds, Midland Road		
70016	DFGH	Crewe, Basford Hall		
70017	DFGI	Tilbury	4M51, Tilbury - Daventry	Freightliner
70018	DFGI	Eastleigh		
70019	DFGI	Ditton	6K74, Ditton - Basford Hall	Freightliner
70020	DFGI	Lawley Street	0Z73, Lawley Street - Peterborough	Route learner

70014 Freightliner's 'Powerhaul' Class 70 No.70014 (above) passes Ebbw Junction, Newport, on 10th March with 4V22, 09:30 Fiddlers Ferry - Cardiff Pengam coal empties, which usually run to Stoke Gifford for stabling, pending the next coal run. In the yard, DBS Class 66/0 No.66100 is stabled, awaiting its next turn of duty.   **Jamie Squibbs**

After working in to the power station on 6Z22, ex-Liverpool Bulk Import Terminal, No.70014 (below) is seen leaving Toton in good light on 25th January with the return coal empties, running as 4Z68, Ratcliffe - Crewe. The '70s' working out of Liverpool run to either Ironbridge or Ratcliffe power station.   **Alan Hazelden**

70015 (above) : On 11th January No.70015 makes for a fine sight heading east and past the 'Up Goods Loop' at Halton with 6F02, 12:07 Ellesmere Port - Fiddlers Ferry loaded 'HHAs'. The train is some eight miles from Warrington's Latchford Sidings, where a reversal will take place, so the '70' will be heading the right way to enter the power station.

Fred Kerr

70015

On Monday, 23rd January, No.70015 (above) storms through the cutting at Horbury on the approaches to Healey Mills yard with a late running empty hopper train for Scotland, which is 4S42, 11:09 (MO-Q) Leeds Hunslet Yard - Hunterston.

4S42 is scheduled 'Mondays Only' and doesn't run every week. There was no indication it would run today, let alone with a Class 70 on the front in place of the usual FHH Class 66. Being over two years since the '70s' were introduced, this is the first real revenue earning working by one through the Calder Valley in daylight, and probably the first time the class has actually been over Copy Pit.

Class 70s have only previously been seen on loco movements running between Crewe Basford Hall and Leeds Midland Road, which occasionally include empty hoppers being transferred as well. **Derek Holmes**

(Previous images)

(Page 89) : On 27th March, No.70015 leads a rake of loaded 'Gondolas' along the WCML 'Down Slow' at Heamies Farm, near Norton Bridge, with 6U77, 13:44 (FO) Mountsorrel - Crewe VQ. Despite the paraphernalia of overhead wires and stanchions, impressive shots can be obtained 'under the wires'! The 'VQ' (Virtual Quarry) concept was adopted in January 1999, following a review of infrastructure requirements. Engineers trains would be formed at a handful of 'Local Distribution Centres' ('LDC'), most of which have a 'Virtual Quarry' to stockpile ballast and receive spoil. 'VQs' were set up around the network with three major WCML 'LDCs' - Crewe Basford Hall, Carlisle Yard and Rugby. **Fred Kerr**

70016

(page 88) : In sparkling 'ex-works' condition, No.70016 crosses Coalbrookdale Viaduct on 14th January with 4Z93, the 13:00 Ironbridge - Crewe Basford Hall coal empties, where the wagons will be staged pending a run to Liverpool BKTM for loading.

Coalbrookdale Viaduct is a brick-built structure and has twenty six-arches. The railway which crosses the River Severn was opened in 1864, forming part of a through route from Wellington (via Much Wenlock) to Craven Arms! Track rationalisation took place in October 2006 resulting in the uphill line being taken out of use; the remaining downhill line becoming a 'bi-directional' extension of the existing single line from Madeley Junction. It is possible this line will eventually become a passenger route into the Ironbridge Gorge, when the power station eventually closes. **Mike Hemming**

70017 On 2nd March, No.70017 (above) passes Chelmscote on the WCML hauling a late running 4M54, 10:10 Tilbury - Crewe Basford Hall freightliner, which includes two Class 86/6s Nos.86614 and 86639 (DIT) in the consist. 4M54 is 'booked' for a pair of Class 86/6s, so the two '86s' presumably failed somewhere on route. **Nigel Gibbs**

On 25th April, No.70017 (below) passes Scout Green, Shap, with 6C16, 08:07 (TX) Crewe Basford Hall - Carlisle Yard departmental service, consisting of 'JJA' autoballasters. There are 11 'JJAs' in view and, as these wagons are in 5-vehicle sets, there must be at least 15 wagons in tow. **Keith McGovern**

70018 Just before the clouds put an end to the morning sun, No.70018 (above) passes Bourton (five miles east of Swindon) on 2nd April with a very lightly loaded 4O51, 09:58 Cardiff Wentloog - Southampton freightliner; three days after this image was taken, No.70018 catches fire at Wallers Ash, Micheldever - see below ....

Steven King

On 5th April, No.70018 suffers a serious fire at Wallers Ash while hauling 4O27, 05;40 (MX) Garston - Southampton maritime freightliner. This results in the line being closed for more than two hours while the fire brigade put the fire out. There are serious delays to South West Trains and Cross Country services before Class 66/5 No.66556 is despatched from Southampton to haul the train to its destination. In this view, No.70018 (below) is seen being towed by No.66556 at Shawford, the fire damage visible above the 'er' branding on the body side - No.70018 is scheduled for a return to traffic in October.

Simon Howard

70019 Looking radiant in the morning sunshine, No.70019 (above) passes through Leamington Spa station on 17th April with 4O49, 09:23 (MO) Birch Coppice - Southampton freightliner. The train runs from Crewe Basford Hall on other days of the week and can be hauled by either a Class 70 or Class 66 loco. **David Weake**

No.70019 (below) passes Battledown, west of Basingstoke, where the lines to Southampton and Salisbury diverge. This is a popular vantage point and No.70019 is heading 4O14, 07:00 (MX) Birch Coppice - Southampton freightliner on 21st March. The Flyover carries the 'Up Southampton' main line and the lines which dive underneath are the former London & South Western Railway lines to Andover, Salisbury and further west to Exeter. **Simon Howard**

70020 The last one .... No.70020 (above) heads through Colchester North station on 22nd May with 4M93, 14:36 Felixstowe - Lawley Street freightliner. Colchester's platform 3/4 boasts the longest platform in the UK at 2,034ft, Gloucester comes in second at 1,977ft. A little bit of railway trivia to conclude this section on the new arrivals.
Nigel Gibbs

Currently the newest loco in the UK, No.70020 (below) passes Didcot East Junction on 10th July while working 4O27, 05:40 (MX) Garston - Southampton freightliner. The '70s' share freightliner turns with '66/5s' on the Southampton route and, apart from 4O27 / 4M98 serving Garston, at this time, only 4O22, 01:47 Trafford Park - Southampton is booked Class 70 traction on this route.
Steven Brykajlo

Breaking New Ground

Selective Images

Flyash : West Burton power station despatches flyash to the cement works at Earles and '70s' have started to appear on these trains. On 13th July, Class 70 No.70014 (above) is captured passing Whisker Hill Junction, Retford, with a rake of loaded 'PCAs', running as 6Z08, West Burton - Earles sidings. The line on the right is the 'Down Worksop' which crosses over in the distance and leads to the ECML and Retford High Level station. Whisker Hill Junction is also known as Down Thrumpton West Junctions.   **Alan Padley**

(Overleaf) :

Limestone : Powdered limestone is used in English power stations to trap carbon dioxide and neutralize any acidic gases produced from fuel combustion. Ratcliffe (FHH), Rugeley (FHH), West Burton (FHH) and Fiddlers Ferry (FHH) all receive limestone from Tunstead. Cottam and Ferrybridge (both DBS) receive their supply from Dowlow. Other than Drax, workings tend to be unpredictable, especially West Burton, with the empties generally returning to Barrow Hill. On 27th June, No.70006 (page 96, top) passes Beighton with 6J70, West Burton - Barrow Hill, having run round at Woodhouse, formed of 'HIAs'.   **Alan Padley**

Felixstowe South : Nearly all Freightliner traffic to & from Felixstowe is still in the hands of Class 66/5 locos with the odd Class 70 thrown in the mix from time to time. However, '70s' to Felixstowe South terminal are extremely rare, but 16th March is one such occasion. No.70007 (page 96, bottom) prepares to drop onto 4M73, 21:28 Felixstowe South - Ditton and DBS Class 66/0 No.66095 waits departure time with 4E45, the 22:18 departure to Wakefield.   **Michael Davies** (with permission)

Cement : In June, '70s' are used for driver training at Earles Sidings for the first time and, on the 18th, No.70005 becomes the second of the Class to work to a cement train from the Lafarge cement works to the Dewsbury Terminal - No.70002 being the first! The loaded train runs overnight but the return empties are more sociable - on a bright summer's day, No.70005 (page 97, top) passes Horbury (Millfield Road) hauling 6M89, 09:50 Dewsbury - Earles, on time. approaching Horbury Junction.   **Derek Holmes**

On 25th July, No.70015 (page 97, bottom) becomes the first Class 70 to work over the southern section of the Midland Main Line and is seen passing Radwell with 6L87, 12:37 Earles - West Thurrock loaded cement tanks. Unusually, the train is running on the 'Up Fast' instead of the usual 'Up Slow' line on the far right of this 4-track section. Note Milepost 55, which marks Radwell viaducts.   **Nigel Gibbs**

6J70 ▲   ▼ 4M73

The Future's Bright, the Future's ....

Orange and this is the new colour HNRC (Harry Needle Railroad Company) will adopt for its fleet of locos. The first one to receive the new colours, following its purchase in 2011 and subsequent overhaul, is Class 20 No.20314, which started life as No.D8117 before becoming No.20117 under TOPS, thence No.20314 in November 1998.

HNRC also has Nos.20314 / 20901 / 20905 available for 'spot hire' or contract work, which may include the movement of 'S-Stock'.

On 29th April, No.20314 (above) stands at Barrow Hill, resplendent in its new colours.   **Mick Tindall**

Two To The Sea

On 1st May, DRS Class 20s No.20303 + No.20312 are unusually rostered to haul MoD 'super flask' No.MODA95770 and two escort coaches Nos.9419 and 9428, destined for Devon Dockyard, running as 6Z40, the 05:10 Crewe CLS - Keyham. Nos.20303 + 20312 are first seen passing Kerswell Bridge (above) and then passing through Dawlish (overleaf) along the sea wall.   **Robert Sherwood / Peter Slater**

Exploding into Life

Superb effect and plenty of 'clag' .... DRS unbranded '20s', No.20301 + No.20304 (above), bubble away on a very cold morning at Crewe on 10th December 2011, complete with one empty wagon, creating the illusion of a pair on a flask train; that said, after their hire to GBRf, they'll soon be back on flasks.   **Michael Wright**

'S' Stock Moves

7X09, Old Dalby - Amersham

'Heritage' Class 20s on the main line attracts great interest among enthusiasts and the use of them (4!) on the movement of new 'S-Stock' to Amersham is an ongoing treat for followers of this traction. Two trains per week are scheduled to run until the London Olympics in July and then resuming thereafter.

Traction is initially Nos.20142 / 20189 / 20227 / 20901 / 20905 although these will be changed periodically throughout the year - a selection of these 'choppers' in action now follows ....

(Above) : **Leicester** - On 11th January, 7X09 arrives in Leicester with No.20227 + No.20142 leading a rake of the new stock with No.20901 + No.20905 bringing up the rear. The train is heading for Knighton Junction, where a second reversal will be affected; the first reversal being at Melton Mowbray and two further reversals will take place at Princes Risborough and Aylesbury. The journey from start to finish takes around 12-hours and a sample schedule for 7X09 is shown on Page 104. **David Weake**

(Previous Page) : **Bagworth** - A delightful setting with the sunshine staying out just long enough for a perfect composition. A colourful combination of railfreight grey (red stripe) No.20227 + BR Blue No.20142 head a new rake of London underground stock on 15th April, sandwiched between two bogie tank wagons and Class 20s Nos.20905 +20901 bringing up the rear. **Ross Byers**

(Opposite) : **Rearsby** - On the Melton Mowbray line, Nos.20901 + 20905 (top right) pass Rearsby on 5th March with 7X09, the 11:42 Old Dalby - Amersham. Rearsby is a small village and civil parish in the Charnwood district of Leicestershire, situated on the A607 between Leicester and Melton Mowbray, just south of the River Wreake.

Melton Mowbray - A classic setting .... Nos.20901 + 20905 (bottom right) approach Melton Mowbray station on 11th January; both locos sporting BR Trainload Freight livery of two-tone grey with black doors and window surrounds. The station here was formerly known as Melton Mowbray Town to distinguish it from the now closed Melton Mowbray North on the Great Northern and London & North Western Joint Railway, which closed to regular traffic in 1953. **David Weake (2)**

(Top Left) : Asfordby

On 28th May, BR Blue No.20142 is swapped with Brunswick Green No.20189 and is paired with Railfreight Grey (red stripe and large logo) No.20227.

The colourful combination is seen passing Asfordby on the Old Dalby Test Track, having worked 6M21, Derby Etches Park - Old Dalby.

This line is used for testing new designs of train and lies between Melton Mowbray and Edwalton on the course of the former Midland Railway's route between Kettering and Nottingham, which closed to passengers in 1968. The line is 13.5 miles in length.

In 2001 the test track was leased by Alstom Transport who electrified the former Down line at 25kV AC OHLE to test and commission Class 390 'Pendolino' trains for introduction by Virgin Trains on the WCML.

When Alstom withdrew from train building in the UK, the line was threatened with closure before being leased to Metronet in 2007 in order to test and commission London Underground 'S Stock'.

David Stracey

7X09 - Typical Route

Location	Time	Notes
Old Dalby (Depart)	**11:42**	
Melton Junction	12:12 - 12:27	Pathing
Melton Mowbray	12:20	
Melton Mowbray Down Loop	12:23 - 12:38	Reverse
Melton Mowbray	12:41	
Leicester	13:06	
Knighton Junction	13:11 - 13:33	Reverse
Moira	14:32	
Branston Junction	14:52 - 17:06	Pathing
Wichnor Junction	17:14	
Elford Loop	17:20 - 1810	Pathing
Tamworth High Level	18:18	
Whitacre Junction	18:41	
Water Orton	18:50	
Landor St Junction	19:00 - 1902	Pathing
Tyseley	19:22	
Dorridge Up Passing Loop	19:37 - 19:59	Pathing
Leamington Spa	20:20	
Banbury	20:52 - 22:18	Pathing
Aynho Junction	22:27	
Bicester North	22:41	
Princes Risborough	23:22 - 23:32	Reverse
Aylesbury	23:59 - 00:11	Reverse
Stoke Mandeville	00:21	
Great Missenden	00:35	
Mantles Wood	00:41	
Amersham (Arrive)	**00:45**	

(Centre) : Ketton - When the crossing gates at Ketton close and the westbound starter signal is pulled off, it is presumed the next train to appear will be a GBRf intermodal (4M29).

But no, instead of the chant of an EMD 12N-710G3B-EC, it's the bass rumble of a quartet of English Electric 8 SVT Mk.IIs which break the silence. And, here they come, four 20s (Nos.20901, 20905, 20227 and 20142) on their way from Peterborough to Derby to pick up another train of 'S stock' for delivery to Neasden depot.

Ketton is on the Leicester - Melton Mowbray - Peterborough line, which is still controlled in the main by semaphore signalling. Ketton 'box is one of nine such 'boxes on this 48-mile stretch of track.

Nick Slocombe

New Kids on the 'S' Stock Block ....

HNRC Class 20s, in new orange livery, No.20311 + No.20314 (above) head 'S' stock barrier move 6Z20, the 12:31 West Ruislip - Derby Etches Park on 3rd October and are seen passing Irthlingborough Road, Wellingborough, in T 'n' T mode with No.20096 + No.20107 bringing up the rear. A Class 222 'Meridian' DMU heads away from the camera with 1B51, the 15:03 Nottingham - London St. Pancras - a close call. **Nigel Gibbs**

On 10th October, another pair of Class 20s No.20901 + 20905 (below) make their first outing resplendent in GBRf colours working 7X09, Old Dalby - Amersham 'S' Stock. The pair and are seen standing at Banbury for pathing purposes; Nos.20096 and 20107 are on the rear of the train. At the time, Class 20s on hire to GBRf (Pool GBEE) are Nos.096 / 107 / 142 / 189 / 227 / 311 / 314 / 901 and 905. **Simon Howard**

Torness Flasks

6S43, 06:42 (WO) Carlisle Kingmoor - Torness   2 DRS 37s / 57s

Wednesday, 23rd May. It is a beautiful day in Scotland (Edinburgh, in particular). Glorious sunshine and the rarity of Class 20s on the Torness flasks - the first time in more than four years since a pair of 'choppers' have appeared on this service. Fortunately, two photographers are at hand .....

Selective Images :

On the outward journey, No.20301 'Max Joule 1958 - 1999' + No.20305 (top left) are seen passing Niddrie West Junction with 6S43 en route via Millerhill to join the ECML at Monktonhall Junction. The imposing backdrop is Edinburgh's Arthur's Seat, the main peak of a group of hills which form most of Holyrood Park, and which rise to over 800ft above sea level. **Keith McGovern**

Meanwhile, four minutes earlier, the pair of 'choppers' (bottom left) pass the site of the former Newington station on the Edinburgh Suburban Line, which bypasses Edinburgh Waverley station. **Steven Brykajlo**

Now on the ECML, Nos.20301 + 20305 (above) pass Prestonpans running to Grantshouse 'Up Passenger Loop' to effect a run-round so the flasks can be taken into the nuclear power station. **Keith McGovern**

Having visited Torness and picked up some spent fuel rods, No.20305 (below) now leads on the return journey and is seen leaving Millerhill with 6M50, 15:12 (WO) Torness - Carlisle Kingmoor. The driver makes a friendly wave as the spotless '20s' pass by. **Steven Brykajlo**

Orange on the Move

Following their overhaul and repaint in orange livery, the two HNRC Class 20s are soon put to revenue earning work. On 21st August the '20s' are hired by DCR to collect two barrier vehicles from Derby and continue to Kilmarnock, where they will collect former First Great Western buffet car No.42513, which has been converted for additional seating. On the outward journey, Nos.20311 + 20314 (above) top 'n' tail 5Z20, Washwood Heath - Kilmarnock through Buckshaw, between Chorley and Preston.

The following day, having picked up their payload, Nos.20314 + 20311 (below) double-head 5Z20 and pass Brock on the WCML, 7 miles and 60 chains north of Preston. The '20s' work as far as Washwood Heath, where they are replaced.

Fred Kerr (2)

37075 at Home on KWVR

On 1st April, Class 37/0 No.37075 (above) stands alongside Class 4f No.43924 in Haworth Shed Yard, having been sold and moved to the Keighley & Worth Valley Railway from the Churnet Valley Railway. Built by the London Midland company in 1920, No.43924 is the last surviving true Midland 4F locomotive and is famous for having been the first locomotive to leave Barry Scrapyard at the end of steam.

No.37075 carries split headcode boxes at one end and a flush front at the other. Here, the 'split box' end is on show as No.37075 (below) ambles along GN Straight with the 09:00hrs ex-Oxenhope. **Neil Harvey (2)**

Bienvenido De Nuevo Locomotoras Ingesas De Espana

Welcome back English locos from Spain - after spending some 11 years there, six of the 14 Class 37s originally sent to Spain have come home; all six last seeing use during the construction of a high speed line between Barcelona and Girona before being stored in early 2011 at the state owned ADIF (Administrator of Railway Infrastructures) base of Hostalric.

Unfortunately, since being stored, the six locos have been the victim of local graffiti which masks their Spanish livery. The original 'GIF' livery was a light grey roof, sky/powder blue body, plus a dark blue band (roughly the same size as the gold band on EWS locos) running along the body side - 'GIF' lettering and an 'L' number in white applied to each loco on the dark blue band. However, when GIF became Continental Rail, this GIF identity was removed in favour of small Continental Rail branding applied to the cabside and nose. The respective details of all 14 'Spanish 37s' are:

No.	Pool	Comments	Spanish No.		Previous Nos.	
37702	WZKS	Scrapped	L30		37020	D6720
37703	WZKS		L25		37067	D6767
37714	WZKS		L26	L031	37024	D6724
37716	WZKS		L23	L034	37094	D6794
37718	WZKS		L22	L021	37084	D6784
37799	WZKS	Sold to Sandbach Car & Commercial	L27	L030	37061	D6761
37800	WZKS		L33		37143	D6843
37801	WZKS	Sold to Sandbach Car & Commercial	L29	L032	37173	D6873
37802	WZKS	Scrapped	L32		37163	D6863
37883	WZKS	Sold to Sandbach Car & Commercial	L28	L028	37176	D6876
37884	WZKS		L34		37183	D6883
37885	WZKS	Scrapped	L24	L033	37177	D6877
37888	WZKS	Scrapped	L31	L024	37135	D6835
37899	WZKS	Scrapped	L21	L022	37161	D6861

On 2nd September, the six former Spanish '37s' are seen having arrived back in the UK at Dollands Moor, all of which have been put up for sale by DBS. The '37s' (above) are, from left to right, Nos.37800, 37884, 37714, 37718, 37703, 37716.　**Michael Wright**

97302

'97/3s' work departmental 'trips' off Bescot, usually to Cambrian metals but, on 26th April, No.97302 (top right) is seen on 6O25, 04:42 Bescot Yard - Eastleigh East Yard. It is passing Cholsey Manor, running in the path of 6V27, Hinksey - Eastleigh. **Ian Cuthbertson**

Meanwhile, on 22nd May, No.97302 (middle) passes Ryecroft Junction with a trainload of concrete railway sleepers, which is 7G22, Washwood Heath - Bescot. The loco is coming off the Sutton Park line while the other line goes via Cannock Chase to Rugeley. **David Weake**

37518

Class 37/5 No.37518 returns to the main line after overhaul and repaint in InterCity swallow-livery - a livery the '37' never carried during its BR career. In this view, No.37518 'Fort William / An Gearasdan' (below) heads away from Bridge of Orchy on the WHL on 3rd August with 5Z32, the 03:53 Carnforth - Fort William, consisting of LMS Stanier 'Black Five' No.44871 + support coach No.35517. Ian Riley's No.37518 will remain at Fort William as a standby loco during the 'Jacobite' season, replacing WCRC No.37706. **Jamie Squibbs**

Winter Development Train

A new Winter Development Train built by RVEL at Derby is unveiled by Network Rail in February and will be operated by DRS in Scotland. The train consists of a converted 'YEA' (Perch) wagon, now renumbered (as a 'YXA') 99709594014-1, fitted with four hot air blowers, called 'Munters'. One Munter is situated on each corner of the vehicle controlled by computer in the Mark 2E accommodation coach, No.977869.

The train also includes a generator, steam lances, hot water and other equipment and in heavy snow will follow a snow blower, which will clear any snow drifts ahead of the train. Initially, the train will be based at Inverness, where it arrived for duty on 18th February.

Three other Snow & Ice Treatment Trains have also been constructed for the southern electric lines, which are illustrated later in this edition.

On a beautiful winter's day, 18th February, the 'Snow Train' sets off for Inverness after a layover in Dundee with two new DRS Class 37s top 'n' tailing it.

No.37667 (top right) is seen leading 6Z31, Dundee West Yard - Inverness 'Snow Train' north past Monifieth; No.37688 is on the rear of the consist.

(Centre) : Close up view of 'YXA' No.99.70.9594.014-1 at Dundee on 12th February. **Jim Ramsay (2)**

On 11th February, the new Winter Development Train leaves Derby bound for Scotland. DRS Class 37s No.37510 + No.37087 'Keighley & Worth Valley Railway' (opposite) top 'n' tail the two vehicles, which are seen storming past Derby Plaza, heading south. The train is 6Z30, Derby RTC - Carlisle. **Mick Tindall**

Nos.37667 and 37688 (below) are seen again on 6Z31, Dundee West Yard - Inverness 'Snow Train', this time alongside the River Don between Dyce and Inverurie.

Dave Purser

37059 .... on the Mallaig Extension

During w/c 19th March, GBRf operate a number of autoballaster trains along the Fort William - Mallaig West Highland Line Extension, dropping ballast in a number of locations using a 5-vehicle set of 'JJAs'. The loco is hired-in from DRS and No.37059 is in charge, substituting for No.37688 which developed a fault.

In absolutely beautiful spring weather, it's too good an opportunity to miss this piece of action and four images are included to illustrate No.37059 out & about on 22nd March.   **Lee Marshall (4)**

Selective Images :

(Top Left)   : **Glenfinnan** : 37059 on 6K21, Fort William TC - Arisaig.

(Bottom Left) : **Loch Eilt** : Ballast Drop.

(Above)   : **Polnish** : Ballast Drop.

(Below)   : **Loch nan Uamh** : 37059 on 6K22, Arisaig - Fort William.

It's that time of year again when DRS makes its annual visit to Hull Docks with low level waste for export to Russia. On 5th July Nos.37611 and 37606, working top 'n' tail (above), shatter the peace at Gilberdyke with 6Z30, the 07:30 Carlisle Kingmoor - Hull Hedon Road.

37611 + 37606
6Z30, Carlisle - Hull Docks

The consist is 'PFA' 2-axle flats in the number range DRSL 92703 - BFL 92856, which are housing containers full of low level waste, believed to be contaminated clothing, presumably to be interred somewhere in the Russian wilderness - there is no return payload!   **James Skoyles**

Meanwhile, 12-miles further east, train 6Z30 is nearing journey's end as the tranquility of the Humber Foreshore is broken by the growl of No.37611 (below) as it passes Hessle with the contaminated payload - DRS traction a pleasant change from the usual fare of DBS and FHH Class 66s.   **Syd Young**

"Two's Company ...." On 23rd March, Nos.37229 'Jonty Jarvis' + 37409 'Lord Hinton' + 97301 (DIT) (above) romp up the final couple of miles to Whiteball Summit with 1Q13, the 06:30 St Blazey - Derby RTC, which had earlier visited the Newquay branch. No.37409 is simply hitching a ride. **Mark Walker**

The second DRS powered 'Cruise Saver' of the 2012 season runs on Thursday, 26th April, and encounters numerous motive power problems with the rostered Class 47s (Nos.47818 and 47841), both of which fail. DRS Class 37s, No.37601 + No.37409 (below) come to the rescue at Derby and the duo, atop No.47818, are seen passing through Dorridge with 1Z73, Edinburgh Waverley - Southampton Docks, running 258 minutes late, no doubt to the considerable annoyance and frustration of passengers! **David Weake**

(*Overleaf*) : DRS No.37194 is virtually in meltdown as it slogs its way up the 1 in 75 Beattock bank with 6S36, Dalston -Grangemouth empty tanks on 19th May; 'sheds' No.66097 and No.66100 have failed and are DIT in the consist. The 'tractor' (quite apt, it's only going 15mph!) is on hire to DBS and is making its way from Kingmoor to Inverness as standby for 'The Cathedrals Explorer' on the Kyle line. The loco takes 25 minutes to climb the bank from a standing start at Beattock village. **Mark Walker**

Low Level Waste .... One of the few operational locos in original DRS livery, No.37038 (above) passes Seascale golf course on 12th April with the 'as required' 7C20, 07:56 Sellafield - Drigg LLWR 'trip'.

The Low Level Waste Repository (LLWR) at Drigg has been in operation since 1959, the waste originally being disposed of by tipping into trenches that have been capped off. Following a major upgrade of disposal operations in 1995, the waste is now placed in engineered concrete vaults. Suitable Low Level Waste (LLW) is compacted and placed in containers before being transferred from Sellafield to the LLWR, where it is then placed in the vaults. Drigg also receives LLW from MoD sites, nuclear power stations, hospitals, universities, medical companies and the oil industry.

Flasks : On 25th May, Class 37/5 No.37688 and Class 20/3 No.20309 (previous page) make a fine sight passing Bootle with 6C52, 1605 Heysham - Sellafield loaded flasks; the Heysham flasks are top and tailed to facilitate ease of access at the Heysham terminal. This is the only flask service which runs directly between power station and reprocessing plant in both directions, all other 'FNAs' are staged at either Carlisle or Crewe accordingly.

	Power Station	Empty 'FNAs'	Loaded 'FNAs'
Carlisle	: Hunterston	(6S54)	
	Seaton-on-Tees	(6E44)	
	Torness		(6M98)
Crewe	: Berkeley	(6V73)	(6M56)
	Bridgewater	(6V74)	(6M67)
	Dungeness	(6O62)	(6M95)*
	Sizewell	(6L70)	(6M69)*
	Valley	(6D41)	(6K41)

* The flasks from Dungeness and Sizewell run to Willesden Brent and go forward as 6K51 to Crewe.

Nitric Acid : This is sourced from Middlesbrough on a weekly basis (6Z24, 20:11 (TO) Middlesbrough - Carlisle Kingmoor) and conveyed to Sellafield on a dedicated 6C24, Carlisle Yard - Sellafield service. This super shot taken at 07:20hrs on the morning of 16th May shows No.37194 (opposite) leading 6C24, 05:36 Carlisle - Sellafield acid tanks at St Bees. Additionally in the consist is ex-works Class 20/3 No. 20305 after repainting at Carlisle Kingmoor along with No.37612. This is a positioning move for both locos to later work 6C51, Sellafield - Heysham 'trip'.

The nitric acid is conveyed in RIV bogie tank wagons (Carkind 'TIA') numbered in the 33. 70. 7899. 022 to 038 series. When nuclear power stations produce electricity, plutonium and uranium are left as a by-product. Sellafield reprocesses this by dissolving the plutonium and uranium in nitric acid, which itself produces liquid waste. The plutonium and uranium is recovered and made into fuel. **Nathan Seddon (3)**

Cumbrian 'Tractors'
Flasks / Acid / Waste

Apart from Wagonload 'trips' to Workington Docks, all the traffic on the scenic Cumbrian Coast Line serves the nuclear reprocessing plant at Sellafield and involves three main flows: nuclear flasks, low level waste and nitric acid. These flows are worked by all loco classes in the DRS fleet : '20s', '37s', '57s' and '66s'.

Typical Sellafield traffic (not necessarily '37s')

Flasks

6C22,	Carlisle Kingmoor - Sellafield	loaded FNAs from Torness / Douneray
6C53,	Crewe Coal Sidings - Sellafield	loaded FNAs from various ps
6C46,	Sellafield - Carlisle Kingmoor	empty FNAs for : Torness
		Hunterston
		Seaton-on-Tees
6C51,	Sellafield - Heysham	empty FNAs
6C52,	Heysham - Sellafield	loaded FNAs
6K73,	Sellafield - Crewe Coal Sidings	empty FNAs for various ps
6M22,	Hunterston - Sellafield	loaded FNAs
6M60,	Seaton-on-Tees - Sellafield	loaded FNAs
6S99,	Sellafield - Georgemas Junction	empty FNAs for Torness

Nitric Acid

6C24,	Carlisle Yard - Sellafield	loaded TIAs from Middlesbrough (6M24)
6C42,	Sellafield - Carlisle Yard	empty TIAs for Middlesbrough (6E19)

Low Level Waste

7C20,	Sellafield - Drigg LLWR	loaded PFAs
7C21,	Drigg LLWR - Sellafield	empty PFAs

Lowestoft Air Show Specials

This annual event takes place in June and is, in fact, the 17th Lowestoft Seafront Air Festival and the first one to be held over a weekend - 23rd & 24th June. Several additional train services are laid on to get visitors to Lowestoft, including loco-hauled services utilising two sets of stock and DRS traction, which are: Class 37/4s No.37419 and No.37425 plus Class 47/8s No.47828 and No.47841, working top 'n' tail. The full diagrams are:

Saturday, 23rd June - Set 1 :

5G92, 08:34 Norwich Crown Point - Norwich
5G91, 10:28 Lowestoft - Norwich
1G93, 16:15 Lowestoft - Norwich
1G95, 18:20 Lowestoft - Norwich

1G92, 09:28 Norwich - Lowestoft
1G94, 11:25 Norwich - Lowestoft
5G96, 17:14 Norwich - Lowestoft
5G95, 19:16 Norwich - Norwich Crown Point

Set 2 :

5G64, 09:43 Norwich Crown Point - Norwich
5G63, 11:26 Lowestoft - Norwich Crown Point
1G97, 17:45 Lowestoft - Norwich

1G64, 10:25 Norwich - Lowestoft
5G94, 16:30 Norwich Crown Point - Lowestoft
5G99, 18:54 Norwich - Norwich Crown Point

Sunday, 24th June - Set 1 :

5G94, 09:47 Norwich Crown Point - Norwich
1G93, 15:40 Lowestoft - Norwich
1G95, 18:15 Lowestoft - Norwich

1G94, 10:40 Norwich - Lowestoft
5J96, 16:31 Norwich - Lowestoft
5G95, 19:19 Norwich - Norwich Crown Point

Three images from Saturday, 23rd June .... the first sees Class 37/4 No.37419 (above) passing Haddiscoe with 1G93, the 16:15 Lowestoft - Norwich (Class 47/8 No.47841 out of sight on the rear) running alongside the River Waveney, seven miles into its journey. Note the stack of new wooden sleepers waiting to be laid.

 (Opposite) : Class 37/4 No.37425, the former 'Concrete Bob', passes Reedham Junction on the approach to Reedham station with a return ECS, running as 5G63, 11:26 Lowestoft - Norwich Crown Point. This junction is where the single line from Great Yarmouth via Berney Arms joins the Lowestoft - Norwich line.

No.37419 (below) is crossing Reedham Swing Bridge with DVT No.82114 behind the loco with another air show ECS, 5G91, 10:28 Lowestoft - Norwich and Class 47/8 No.47828 on the rear. This is the return of the first loco hauled special (1G92) of the morning. The Victorian swing bridge across the River Yare was commissioned in the 1840's to allow passage of wherry boats, which were too tall to pass under conventional bridges. The bridge is operated from the 1904 Reedham Swing Bridge signal box. **Nigel Gibbs (3)**

1Qs : The distinctive Network Rail yellow testing vehicles are now commonplace across the railway network with DRS Class 37s visiting areas of the country not usually blessed with such traction, offering the chance to seek out interesting photographic opportunities. On Wednesday, 8th February, No.37604 (above) hauls 1Q13, 13:00 St Blazey - Bristol St Phillips Marsh Radio Survey Train over Blatchford Viaduct on Wednesday, 8th February. The viaduct is near Ivybridge on the GWML between Totnes and Plymouth. **Robert Sherwood**

10 minutes after leaving Liskeard, No.37682 (below) comes into view descending the 1 in 40 incline to arrive at Coombe Junction, where the shunter will change the points so the train can reverse and head off on the line on the right to Looe. Behind the camera is the tiny halt of Coombe Junction, beyond which is the short 'freight only' line to Moorswater. The '37' is on a circular 1Q13, Plymouth - Plymouth Laira trip. **Nathan Seddon**

A rather unusual combination .... Class 97/3 No.97302 and Class 31/1 No.31106 (above) top 'n' tail 2Q88, the 06:01 Doncaster West Yard - Doncaster TMD test train, which is covering various parts of east and central Yorkshire on 14th May. The ensemble is passing through Horbury Cutting, after a reversal at Healey Mills upon arriving from Hull. The test train was scheduled for a Network Rail Class 150 unit - what a shame!   **Nathan Seddon**

Here, No.37605 + 37608 (below) work top 'n' tail along the 'freight only' former Great Central line at Bessamer Bridge, Rotherham, which links Woodburn Jct. and Rotherham Central Jct, running as 2Q88, Doncaster West Yard - Derby RTC on 7th June. The view is dominated by the Magna Science Adventure Centre, located in a disused steel mill in the Templeborough district of Rotherham. The site is formerly home to the Steel, Peech and Tozer steel works (also known as Steelos) which closed in 1993.   **Alan Padley**

Alcan Derailment

19:05 hrs .... **28th June**

6S45, 06:35 North Blyth - Fort William, comprising GBRf Class 66/7 No.66734 'Eco Express', 3 empty 'PCA' wagons and 21 loaded 'PCAs' strike a boulder and derail beside Loch Treig on the West Highland Line between Corrour and Tulloch.

The loco ploughs down the slope and comes to rest away from the railway on a ledge on the slope. Fortunately, the driver is not injured.

The leading three wagons come to rest on their side parallel to the railway line. It is believed that a boulder is likely to have become dislodged during a landslide; heavy rain in the period preceding the accident is thought to be a factor.

It is believed No.66734 will not be recovered for repair.

In happier times - in fact, the day before the derailment - No.66734 'Eco Express' (above) approaches County March summit with 6E45, Fort William - North Blyth alumina empties.　　**David Stracey**

The other three images depict the final resting place of No.66734, inclusive of a view of the landslip, which was the cause of the derailment following torrential rain.　　**Dave Purser (3)**

On 1st May, No.67003 (left) approaches Craven Arms with 1W91, 16:15 Cardiff Central - Holyhead and the junction for the 'token' controlled 'Heart of Wales' Line to Llandeilo Jct.

Stuart Chapman

On 27th March, No.67002 (below) hauls the slightly late 1W91 'WAG' express, which is seen passing Ponthir. This is a popular spot, just north of Caerleon (Newport) where photographers can enjoy good shots of northbound services, from early afternoon.

Jamie Squibbs

'WAG' EXPRESSES GO '67'

In December 2011, Class 67001 in **Arriva Trains Wales** un-branded livery arrives from Crewe to carry out route learning duties. This loco will replace the '57/3s' on the Cardiff - Holyhead trains in March, along with sister locos No.67002 and No.67003.

Class 57/3 No.57316 is the last of the class to work 1W91 on 23rd March and 1V31 on the 26th, the 'WAG' Express diagram having swapped traction to Class '67s':

    1V31, 05:32 Holyhead - Cardiff   1W91, 16:15 Cardiff - Holyhead

DB Schenker's Arriva Blue liveried, but unbranded, No.67002 becomes the first 'skip' to work 1W91 on 26th March and the first '67' to work 1V31 on 27th March.

1W91

Here we have two shots of No.67003 on 1W91, the 16:15 Cardiff Central - Holyhead express working along the North Wales Coast on 15th and 16th May, respectively. The first image records No.67003 (above) approaching Abergele & Pensarn and the second shows No.67003 (below) crossing Foryd Viaduct, which spans the River Clwyd, one mile west of Rhyl.

David Weake (2)

SPECIAL TRAINS

(Top Left) :
'YXA' No.99.70.9594.012-5.
Ashford West, 28th January.

(Centre) :
'ZZA' No.99.70.9592.001-0.

(Top Right) :
This is Class 57/3 No.57312 accelerating away from Ashford West with 7Z99, the 14:05 Tonbridge West Yard - Tonbridge West Yard 'snow train' with No.57306 bringing up the rear.

The train is on the 'Up Fast' line heading for Tonbridge and the lines leading off to the left behind the two signals are for Maidstone East.

(Bottom Right) :
The same train is seen again, this time passing Five Oak Green between Paddock Wood and Tonbridge.   **Edward Clarkson**

(Below) :
Close up view of Network Rail Class 57/3 No.57312, seen at Eastleigh on 29th March, having arrived with 1Z57, the 13:45 'snow train' from Tonbridge. In November 2011, Network Rail took six '57/3s' from Virgin Trains for use on various duties, including snow trains.

Richard A. Jones (4)

South-East Snow Train

Three Snow & Ice Treatment Trains have been built by RVEL, Derby, for southern electric lines and have been moved to Tonbridge. Each train is top 'n' tailed by Network Rail Class 57/3s with a snowplough at each end and wagons holding generators and de-icing modules in the middle. The consist is:

'ZZA' + Class 57/3 + 'YXA' + 'YXA' + 'YXA' + 'YXA' + Class 57/3 + 'ZZA'

The snowplough ('ZZA') is a converted 'SPA' wagon, fitted with an additional 21 tonne weight on the top, and the wagons sandwiched in between the two Class 57/3 locos are 'YXAs' converted from 'YEA' long welded rail carriers, which carry the de-icing equipment.

Standing under the impressive trainshed canopy at Southport, No.73107 (above) waits to leave for the run to Wigan Wallgate after No.73138 (below) had brought 2Q78, Wigan LIP - Hooton into the terminus. This station receives Merseyrail services from Liverpool along with Northern Rail trains from Manchester (Victoria and Piccadilly) via Wigan Wallgate. **Fred Kerr / Lee Marshall**

In February, Class 73s No.73107 ' Redhill 1844-1994' + No.73138 find themselves well off their normal patch working a Network Rail measurement train around the Merseyrail system. This, combined with night running, is an opportunity not to be missed for a couple of intrepid photographers during 14th and 15th February.

No.73138 (above) tops No.73107 on rear of 2Q78, Wigan L.I.P - Hooton and is standing at Ellesmere station, prior to leaving for the four mile run to Hooton, photographed 5-minutes before midnight on 15th February.

Having reached its destination, 2Q78 takes a breather and No.73107 (below) sits waiting time at Hooton, prior to departure on a circular trip, this time running as 2X78, Hooton - Hooton.   **Lee Marshall (2)**

SNCF Comes to London

 The prospect of a network of high speed freight trains carrying express parcels and other premium consignments across Europe moves a step closer on 21st March, when a demonstration train from Lyon Saint-Exupéry and Paris Charles-de-Gaulle arrives at London's St Pancras International station.

The trial run was organised by the EuroCarex consortium, which includes SNCF, Eurotunnel, Air France, La Poste, FedEx and airport operators in Paris, Amsterdam, Liège and Lyon. The UK element was co-ordinated by GB Railfreight and High Speed 1 Ltd. Loading and unloading being handled by SNCF Geodis subsidiary Geoparts Rail Solutions.

The demonstration run features set 951, one of the three dedicated TGV trainsets which La Poste has been using to carry mail between Paris, Mâcon and Cavaillon since 1984, which unfortunately has to be towed due to the TVM not being configured for use in the Channel Tunnel or HS1. The speed range and headways are apparently configured differently for the tunnel, and domestic French sets will get an emergency brake code if they venture onto Eurotunnel tracks. The train leaves Lyon Saint-Exupéry at 16:42hrs on 20th March 20, arriving at St Pancras the next morning.

Selective Images :

(Top Left) : The two Eurotunnel Mak locos No.0004 and No.0005 are seen just outside London St Pancras International on 21st March, prior to hauling the SNCF postal TGV back to France. Under TOPS, these locos are numbered 21904 and 21905, respectively.   **Robin Morel**

(Bottom left) : French National Railways, TGV (Train a Grande Vitesse) Postal unit No 951 stands at Platform 5 at St Pancras International after arriving from Lyon. In the background, the five Olympic rings are proudly displayed for all to see to mark the London 2012 Olympics.   **Nigel Gibbs**

(Above) : Nos.0005 and 0004 pass a couple of happy snappers at Stratford International as TGV 951 emerges into the sunlight from CTRL Tunnel 1 on 21st March.   **Michael Groom**

(Below) : Having arrived with 6Z02, St. Pancras - Singwell, the train sits in Singwell Loop awaiting passage through the Channel Tunnel.   **Ian Cuthbertson**

56312
5Z56,
Kilmarnock - Laira

On 26th June, DCR Class 56 No.56311 takes some buffet cars back to Plymouth having been modified to provide more seats. Whilst poor light disappoints the photographer, the day does provide some unscheduled excitement ....

5Z56 Timeline :

(10:17hrs) : No.56312 (top left) crosses Metal Bridge, Carlisle, running 10 minutes late, due to continual loss of power.

(11:42hrs) : Having travelled this far, No.56312 (centre) sits in Eden Valley 'Up Goods Loop' failed. Fortunately, a friendly bystander kindly provides a 'taxi' service to take the train driver to DRS Kingmoor to fetch a rescue loco ....

(13:33hrs) : The cavalry arrives, DRS Class 37/6 No.37612 ....

(14:17hrs) : On the move again, No.37612 (below) on full bore drags failed No.56312 and 5Z56, Kilmarnock - Laira past Harrison sidings (Shap) in driving rain and running 3hrs late. **Guy Houston (3)**

The Elizabethan

King's Cross - Edinburgh
55009

25th July 2012

To celebrate the Coronation of Queen Elizabeth II, British Railways changed the name of 'The Capitals Limited' to 'The Elizabethan'; its first runs were on Monday, 29th June 1953, and then each summer, until the end in 1961, when the last steam hauled runs were made.

This famous train ran non-stop between London and Edinburgh in both directions and only corridor-tender fitted Gresley Class A4 4-6-2 Pacifics could be used, provided by King's Cross shed and Haymarket.

From 1962, the 'Deltics' took over and, whilst non-stop to passengers, 'The Elizabethan' stopped briefly at Newcastle for a crew change. So, 2012 marks the 50th Anniversary since the first 'Deltic' worked 'The Elizabethan', quite fitting in Diamond Jubilee year too!

On Wednesday, 25th July 2012, Deltic No.D9009 'Alycidon' sets out from London King's Cross with her first main line passenger train for nine years, resplendent in original colours, heading north down the ECML to Edinburgh, picking up passengers at Peterborough, York and Darlington. A1 4-6-2 Pacific No.60163 'Tornado' will head the return leg to London.

Before the sun is able to rise above the buildings, D9009 (55009) 'Alycidon' (top right) sits at the head of 1Z55, the 06:50 King's Cross - Edinburgh Waverley - 'The Elizabethan' - on 25th July.   **Guy Houston**

Meanwhile, just under 50-miles out of 'KX', 1Z55 is already running about 30 minutes late, as the DPS and former Finsbury Park Deltic No.D9009 'Alycidon' (above) passes Tempsford. It looks superb with its rake of blood and custard MK1s in tow.
Nigel Gibbs

66720 / 50044
1Z50, Cardiff Central - Paignton

On Saturday, 21st July, GBRf lay on a *staff charter* and this one is rather splendid in terms of motive power. The charter features GBRf 'Rainbow Warrior' No.66720 and the Fifty Fund's Class 50 No.50044 'Exeter' running top 'n' tail.

The charter sets off from Cardiff for Paignton, picking up passengers at Newport and Bristol, headed by No.50044. After arriving at Paignton, a mini tour sets off for Plymouth, via a reversal at Newton Abbot, which is open to the public. The train is then turned on the 'Laira Triangle' so that No.50044 could lead out of Paignton on the return journey.

1Z50, Cardiff - Paignton

Location	Timings
Cardiff Central (dep)	**09:15 (50044)**
Newport	09:31
Severn Tunnel Jct.	09:43
Filton Abbey Wood	10:03
Narroways Hill Jct.	10:06
Dr Day's Jct.	10:08
Bristol Temple Meads	10:22
Worle Jct.	10:39
Uphill Jct.	10:41
Bridgwater	10:54
Taunton	11:06
Whiteball	11:17
Tiverton Parkway	11:20
Exeter St Davids	11:35
Dawlish Warren	11:44
Dawlish	11:46
Teignmouth	11:49
Newton Abbot	11:54
Torquay	12:10
Paignton (arr)	**12:17**

1Z51, Paignton - Plymouth

Location	Timings
Paignton (dep)	**12:24 (66720)**
Newton Abbot (arr)	12:46
Newton Abbot (dep)	12:56 **(50044)**
Dainton Tunnel	13:02
Totnes	13:09
Ivybridge	13:24
Hemerden	13:29
Plymouth (arr)	**13:40**

1Z52, Plymouth - Paignton

Location	Timings
Plymouth (dep)	**16:50 (50044)**
Hemerden	17:00
Ivybridge	17:05
Totnes	17:20
Dainton Tunnel	17:28
Newton Abbot (arr)	17:36
Newton Abbot (dep)	17:50 **(66720)**
Paignton (arr)	**18:09**

GBRf Class 66/7 No.66720 (above) passes Hollicombe Cove hauling 1Z52, the 16:50 Plymouth - Paignton charter on Saturday, 21st July, with Class 50 No.50044 DIT on the rear. **Robert Sherwood**

Just Like Old Times .... well, with the exception of the blood & custard liveried coaching stock and a funny coloured loco at the other end, a Class 50 is back on its old haunts on Great Western metals in the west of England. No.50044 'Exeter' (opposite) passes Dawlish displaying a 1Z50 reporting code, which is correct for the 09:15 Cardiff Central - Paignton GBRf staff charter.

On the second leg of the tour, No.50044 (below) storms up Dainton with the 5-coach train with No.66720 bringing up the rear. The '50' performs well until the return journey from Plymouth when the loco suffers from overheating and leaks oil. Consequently, the train is diverted via Bristol Parkway to allow No.66720 to haul the train to Cardiff. **Mark Walker (2)**

6X39

Dollands Moor - Longsight

With a sharp increase in passenger numbers, Virgin Trains recognise the need to create extra capacity in the WCML fleet of Class 390 'Pendolinos'.

This involves increasing the capacity by a combination of new train sets and also lengthening the existing train sets to 11 cars. The first new set was delivered via Dollands Moor to Edge Hill in July 2011.

Due to the closure of the Washwood Heath works, any additional vehicles must be manufactured in Alstom's Savigliano factory in Italy and moved to the UK via the Channel Tunnel. The new coaches are being transferred to Longsight TMD, where the entire Pendolino fleet is allocated (ALSTOM, Manchester Traincare Centre), where heavy maintenance can be carried out; Longsight has a hoist on which an entire Pendolino set can be lifted.

The additional coaches are being transferred from Dollands Moor to Longsight by way of train 6X39, hauled by a Colas Rail Class 66/8 loco, and a selection of images is featured here.

31st May : Colas Rail Class 66/8 No.66848 (above) emerges from under Earls Court with new 'Pendolino' trailers, running as 6X39, 05:35 Dollands Moor - Longsight. On the right, the London Underground District Line from Kensington Olympia to Earls Court drops down and passes underneath the West London Line, the latter being an important inter-regional freight artery.   **John Hurst**

20th July : Breaking the procession of Class 66/8s, Class 47/7 No.47739 'Robin of Templecombe' (top) works another 6X39 service of 'Pendo' coaches bound for Longsight. The '47' is approaching Swanley on the 'Up Chatham Fast' line, heading for the suburbs of south London.   **Ian Cuthbertson**

23rd June : Colas Rail Class 66/8 No.66850 (above) heads 6X39, 05:35 Dollands Moor - Longsight, just south of Otford station before Otford Junction. The consist on this occasion, including 'barrier' wagons, is:

87.4145.200 - (9)68920 - (9)65320 - (9)68919 - (9)65319 - (9)68918 - (9)65318 - (9)68917 - (9)65317 - 87.4145.201

Alan Hazelden

In the north west, lousy weather is the order of the day for the 'FM Meet' at Crewe Basford Hall, though typical of the summer. Here, the photographer gets soaked, securing this atmospheric shot of No.66850 (below) arriving with 6X39, 05:40 Dollands Moor - Longsight with trailers for '390s' 20 / 19 / 18 and 17. The train is drawing to a check on the independent lines to the West of the yard.　　　　**John Hurst**

'**Grime & Shine'** : Well, not so much of a new livery, but can you see the present one? Is it a case of financial hardship, lack of care or simply the effect of hard graft working seasonal RHTT trains, that locos are allowed to get so filthy, save for keeping the loco number clear of grime to aid loco recognition.

On 2nd December 2011, the East Midlands RHTT (3J88, 21:34 Toton - Toton) passes East Holmes, Lincoln, with filthy ECR 'shed' No.66123 (above) leading. The train is crossing the River Witham. **Nigel Gibbs**

Meanwhile, on 10th November 2011, Class 97/3 No.97304 (below) waits at Shrewsbury with 3S71, Crewe - Machynlleth water cannon; the relevant details having been cleaned for all to see. **Mike Hemming**

59201 (above) : Although only three Class 66/0s (Nos.66097 / 101 / 152) carry DBS corporate red out of a fleet size of 250, all five Class 59/2s have been so adorned. Following No.59206 in 2009, three years later No.59201 is repainted, which is seen on 2nd July (now minus its nameplates) stabled overnight in Acton Yard pending its next turn of duty, 7A23 loaded stone to Brentford.   **Craig Adamson**

66414 (below) : Following the loss of the Tesco contract by DRS to DBS, No.66414 (formerly 'James the Engine') and No.66411 'Eddie the Engine' lose their Stobart branding and transfer to Freightliner. No.66411 moves to Poland (DFEP pool) and No.66414 goes into the DFIN pool, the latter is seen here at Battledown, Basingstoke, on 9th June heading 4027, 05:40 (MX) Garston - Southampton freightliner.   **Simon Howard**

66434 Class 66/4 No.66434 transfers to DRS following the demise of Fastline and, in December 2011, is outshopped in a brand new colour scheme on behalf of DRS customer Malcolm Ltd, Grangemouth, and striking it looks too! Its first outing is on 21st January and No.66434 (above) is seen on 4A13, 12:20 Grangemouth - Aberdeen intermodal near Inchyra, Perth.   **Alastair Blackwood**

67026 On 3rd October, No.67026 'Diamond Jubilee' (below) runs top 'n' tail with No.67029 'Royal Diamond' on the OHLE test train 1Q18, 12:32 Crewe - Crewe via London Euston, seen here on the 'Down Main' at Blisworth. Note the three EWS livery Mk2s in the consist which had gone north as ECS from Wembley behind No.37603 five days previously. As for No.67029, gone are the striking EWS 'three beast heads' on the body side, replaced by a standard, rather bland 'DB' logo.   **Nigel Gibbs**

Staying in Scotland, No.66434 (above) is seen again, but this time on 4th October crossing Slochd Viaduct on the Highland Line heading south with 4D47, 13:23 Inverness - Mossend intermodal. DRS are the main traction providers for internal Scottish intermodal traffic, running regulary to Aberdeen and Inverness, plus Elderslie, although the latter flow is erratic to say the least.   **John Tomlin**

DBS repaint Class 67 No.67026 in silver to celebrate Her Majesty The Queen's Diamond Jubilee, complete with Union Jack flag. Alongside is a version of the official emblem of the Diamond Jubilee, designed by 10-year old Katherine Dewar from Chester. On 14th June, No. 67026 (below) passes Bygrave on the Hitchin - Cambridge line with an ECS in connection with the Queen's 2012 Diamond Jubilee tour.   **Nigel Gibbs**

Greater Anglia

Anglia 'IANA' pool, No.90009 'Diamond Jubilee' (above), newly repainted in celebration of the Queen's Diamond Jubilee, speeds south at Dunston on 23rd June with 1P23, the 09:00 Norwich -Liverpool Street; the loco's second trip of the day to the Capital. **Nathan Seddon**

Stratford 47 Group

Class 47 No.47580 'County Of Essex' (below) climbs past Blea Moor on 2nd June with the 'Settle & Carlisle Statesman' - 1Z36, the 06:05 Newport - Carlisle and, despite the dull conditions and low cloud cover, the '47' still makes for an impressive sight. Interestingly, both former Union Jack '47s' No.47163 and No.47164 survive, albeit in the guise of WCRC No.47787 and Network Rail No.57305, respectively. **Neil Harvey**

Her Majesty The Queen's Diamond Jubilee

Many British railway companies and loco owners are getting in to the spirit of the Queen's Diamond Jubilee by adopting special liveries. As we have already seen, DB Schenker repaint Class 67 No.67026 in a silver livery, which is named 'Diamond Jubilee' by the Queen at Manchester Victoria station on 23rd March as she starts her tour of the country.

These two pages illustrate three more commemorations, which are as equally pleasing on the eye. Perhaps, the most striking and memorable is the Stratford 47 Group's decision to adorn No.47580 'County of Essex' with Union Jacks in the style of those carried by Stratford TMD's Class 47/0s, No.47163 and No.47164, which were so adorned to commemorate the Queen's Silver Jubilee.

First Great Western

These images depict First Great Western's contribution by adorning Class 43 power car No.43186 in Jubilee colours and lettering.

(Top) : A 'panned' shot shows the celebrity power car No.43186 tailing 1B63, the 17:15 London Paddington - Carmarthen on 14th May speeding through Bishton. **Jamie Squibbs**

(Above & Centre) : Close up view of the decoration adorning No.43186, photographed on 18th June at Paignton on the rear of 1A82, the 11:06 departure to London Paddington. **Robert Sherwood (2)**

"LEST WE FORGET"

More than 2,000 people come together on 2nd June at the start of the 'Railfest' exhibition at York for the naming of Class 91 No.91119 'Battle of Britain Memorial Flight', which includes a flypast by a Spitfire, Hurricane and Lancaster bomber 'Phantom of the Ruhr'.

Several celebrities attend, including Squadron leader Ian Smith and retired Squadron leader Stuart Reid, who recount many wartime stories to set the scene for the event. TV presenter Carol Vorderman, a long-standing supporter of the RAF BBMF, presses the button to release the curtain covering the new livery, designed by graphic designer Paul Gentleman.

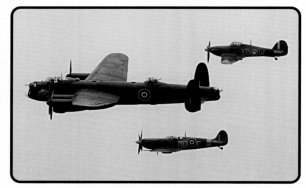

This livery must surely be regarded as one of the most striking and innovative of any seen to date - perhaps, the best ever and the accompanying images surely prove the point!

No.91110 also carries a plaque in recognition of attaining a British loco speed record of 162mph, set on 17th September 1989, just south of Little Bytham during a test run on Stoke Bank. A DVT was leading.

Selective Images :

(Top Left) : No.91110 'Battle of Britain Memorial Flight' nameplate, with RAF BBMF crest. **Nigel Gibbs**

(Centre Left) : BBMF flypast at York. **Carl Gorse**

(Below Left) : East Coast Class 91 No.91110 waits in platform 7 at London King's Cross station on 6th June to work 1S09, the 09:00 service to Edinburgh Waverley. **Nigel Gibbs**

(Above) : Close up of No.91110 body side BBMF emblem and Lancaster bomber. **Nigel Gibbs**

(Below) : The other side, a montage of WW11 fighters - Spitfire and Hurricane. **Neil Harvey**

At Sunset

Warning
Do not trespass
on the Railway
Penalty £1000

(Above) - (17:44hrs) : Looking back towards Didcot, FHH 'Shanks'-liveried No.66522 approaches Steventon Causeway on 21st March with 4V11, (MWFO) 10:49 Washwood heath - Fairwater Yard departmental service conveying concrete sleepers on 'YXA' Network Rail sleeper carriers.

(Top Left) - (18:08hrs) : This is what the photographer was after - the sun directly down the tracks and a train coming out of it - nearly, but not quite. Firstly, on 21st March, an unidentified HST heads away from the camera at Steventon Causeway with 1B63, the 17:43 London Paddington - Carmarthen.

(Bottom Left) - (18:16hrs) : Just 8 minutes after the first attempt, the sun has already crossed the sky and another HST is the nearest to a train coming out of the sun, as it heads towards Didcot with 1L82, the 16:55 Cardiff Central - London Paddington - perhaps, another try on another day! **Stephen Dance (3)**

"Here Comes The Rain Again"

A rare positioning move occurs on 14th of June when 'Slim Jim' Class 33/2 No.33207 (above) stands at a very wet Doncaster Up Decoy yard after arriving with a Kirow crane on 6T71, 22:00 engineer's trip from Glaisdale. The possession from the previous weekend on the Esk Valley line had overrun and the crane was urgently required for the following weekend on a possession train from Bescot. No other operator could source a loco and so the 'Crompton' was summoned after being on hand at the York 'Railfest'. **Nathan Seddon**

In pouring rain, perseverance is rewarded with a fine shot of Class 92 No.92016 (below) passing through Caledonian Road on the North London Line, 13th February, with an additional 6X48, 13:48 Dagenham - Wembley seasonal service running in conjunction with the new vehicle registration change. It is very rare to see a Class 92 on the NLL, especially in daylight, and these trains are usually '90'-hauled. **John Hurst**

Rail 'Riding' in YORKSHIRE

Millwood Tunnel : Waiting patiently, ready for action .... the photographer manages to catch Class 47/8 No.47826 (right), with 'Scarborough Spa Express' branding on the body side, emerging from the west portal of Millwood Tunnel, Todmorden.

The '47' is taking the Copy Pit line at Hall Royd Junction on 6th May with 5Z86, 11:45 Peterborough - Preston ECS. Surely, it's about time WCRC got rid of this mobile advertising and, at the same time, adopt a more invigorating livery for its loco fleet.

Todmorden is the historic county boundary between Yorkshire and Lancashire, marked by the River Calder and its tributary, Walsden Water, which runs through the centre of the town. **Neil Harvey**

(Selective Images)

(Overleaf)

(Page 154)

Crimble Viaduct : With a scattering of snow on the hillside above Slaithwaite, FHH No.66519 (top) crosses Crimble Viaduct on 5th April with 6M07, 11:09 (TThO) Roxby - Pendleton empty 'GMC' Binliner, which runs to Dean Lane on the other three days of the week.. Crimble Viaduct should not be confused with Slaithwaite Viaduct, which is less than half-a-mile further west of here. **Lee Marshall**

Ferrybridge : The cooling towers of Ferrybridge power station loom above 'shed' No.66056 (bottom) as it passes over the bridge spanning the River Calder at Brotherton with a rake of 'MBA' 'Monster' bogie box wagons on 27th July. The train is 6N07, 06:45 (MX) Thoresby - Butterwell. Perseverance pays off, as this 'shot' involved climbing a 6 foot wall, balancing on top while holding onto a fence with one hand and shooting with the other - well done in achieving a great result! **Alan Padley**

(Page 155)

Lockwood Viaduct : DBS Class 67 No.67029 'Royal Diamond' (top) leads 1Z81, the 14:13 Southport - King's Cross 'Sandgrounder' charter across Lockwood Viaduct, Huddersfield, on 31st March, with No.67005 'Queen's Messenger' on the rear. With not many loco-hauled trains down the Penistone Branch, this shot just had to be done.

Lockwood Viaduct was built across the Holme Valley between 1846 - 1849 for the Huddersfield and Penistone Railway; it is 1,428ft long, 136ft high with 32 arches, built with stone obtained from two cuttings immediately to the south. Interestingly, the 13 miles of track between Huddersfield and Penistone boasts 6 tunnels (10,281' in total), 4 major viaducts and 30 bridges. **Neil Harvey**

Elland Tunnel : Classic location, classic engine ....LMS Princess Coronation 4-6-2 Pacific No.46233 'Duchess of Sutherland' (bottom) emerges from the east portal of Elland Tunnel with 1Z80 the 06:55, Crewe - Scarborough, 'The Scarborough Flyer', on 3rd August. The tour had been originally advertised to run via the Standedge route but was re-routed via the Calder Valley main line.

On 3rd March, No.46233 was rolled out in Brunswick green livery, as used by British Railways during the early 1950's, at Butterley following major overhaul. **Neil Harvey**

6M07 ▲   ▼ 6N07

1Z81 ▲   ▼ 1Z80

Selby Swing Bridge : The swing bridge was built for the North Eastern Railway between 1850 – 1899 and carries the railway line from Selby to Hull across the River Ouse. It is on what was once part of the East Coast Main Line and Selby swing bridge was a major bottleneck, until the ECML was rerouted to avoid the Selby Coalfield in 1983. The original route north of Selby (Barlby Junction to York) closed but the southern section remains in operation, used by passenger services to Doncaster and London.

Selective images :

(Above) : Wide angle view of the section of bridge which spans the River Ouse.

(Below) : Close up, side-on view, of the control tower which operates the bridge, housed directly above the railway line. This is also the 'swing span' which moves to allow the passage of boats, moving the whole line with it - hence why this used to be such a bottleneck section of the ECML.   **Alan Padley (2)**

(Opposite) : Looking at the swing bridge control tower head-on from Selby station, Class 47/4 No.47580 'County of Essex' is about to cross the river and enter the station on 7th April with 1Z45, Scarborough - Carlisle, the 'Settle Carlisle Thunderer' charter.   **Alan Hazelden**

Technological Wonders

Wind Turbines : The skyline at King's Dyke, between Peterborough and Whittlesea, is dominated by the brick works chimney stacks and wind turbines, which power local factories, like McCains oven chips. GBRf Class 66/7 No.66728 'Institution of Railway Operators' (above) heads west on St. David's Day with 4E33, 11:20 Felixstowe South - Doncaster intermodal. Only one of the wind turbines is turning, the others are feathered. In 2007, Fenland District Council gave planning consent for a single wind turbine to be located here and this now forms part of a larger Wind Farm.

Nick Slocombe

Forth Railway Bridge : For the first time in over a decade, this magnificent structure is scaffold-free, thanks to new painting techniques and it will be at least 25 years before it needs to be repainted again! On 23rd April, a miniscule-looking Class 67 No.67016 (below) heads towards North Queensferry with 2L69, the 17:21 Edinburgh - Cardenden. The Forth Bridge is a cantilever design, opened on 4 March 1890, 8,296 ft in length and has a clearance of 151ft above the water - it is a Category A-listed bridge connecting Lothians with Fife and is "the one immediately and internationally recognised Scottish landmark".

Stuart Chapman

'Off The Peg'

Barnetby : This is one of the most photographed locations in the country, when it comes to semaphore signals and it is clear to see why .... this composition sees a long train of petroleum tanks coming off the Lincoln line at Wrawby Junction in perfect light. On 14th September, the photographer manages to get this shot having tried before - Class 60 No. 60063 (above) glistens in the morning sun as it picks its way across Wrawby Junction with 6E46, 04:35 Kingsbury - Lindsey.

A great end to a great day's photography - a superb sunset - looking west, No.66100 (below) brings 6D49, (MFX) 13:55 Ferrybridge - Lindsey empty bogie tanks through Barnetby on 24th November 2011, under an awesome sky. (Canon EOS 450D .... f/7 .... 1/640th sec .... ISO400)

Syd Young (2)

The Wider Picture

Kings Sutton Floods : At the time, heavy rainfall causes flooding in this area. Although the waters have receded slightly, the railway is still a virtual causeway across the water meadows, as can be seen here with WCRC Class 47s No.47245 and 47760 (above) running in top 'n' tail formation and heading north on 6th May with 5Z76, Southall – Derby empty coaching stock move. It was amusing to hear southbound trains still sounding a warning for users of the foot crossing situated halfway down the train! The road bridge here is a popular spot and is especially good for shots of northbound train services, mid-afternoon onwards. The bridge is located on Banbury Lane, which is off the main A4260 Oxford – Banbury road at Adderbury, which goes on to the village of Kings Sutton.

Stephen Dance

Snow Capped Peaks : East Coast HST No.43300 (above) storms towards Slochd summit with 1S15, the 12:00 London King's Cross - Inverness 'Highland Chieftain' on 19th May where, in the background, snow still lingers in deep abundance on the snow capped Cairngorms mountain range to the East / South of Aviemore. The Slochd Summit is a mountain pass on the Highland Main Line Railway and A9 road between Inverness and Aviemore, both having a sign marking the spot - the railway reaches 1,315ft above sea level, while the road is at a height of 1,328ft. Slochd Summit is the second highest place on the route from Inverness to Perth - the Pass of Drumochter at 1,500ft is higher and bleaker. Slochd is pronounced "slochk".

Mark Walker

Winter Wonderland : There's heavy snow around Peak Forest, very little traffic is passed on the five hour out & back trip in the '4 x 4', the cars and lorries that were passed were all stuck. Is this madness or does the result justify the means! Class 60 No.60065 'Spirit of JAGUAR' (above) sits on the fuel line at Peak Forest on 4th February, with snow lying crisp, deep and even. In the distance, smoke drifts aimlessly into the evening sky from the Tunstead cement and limestone works. **Mick Tindall**

Colours of the Rainbow with beautiful light and shade all around. GBRf's Rainbow liveried Class 66/7 No.66720 (displaying its 'night' side) (below) leans into the curve at Thornwell, powering 6E01, the 17:17 (TO) Cardiff Tidal - Lindsey empty bogie tanks on 1st May. The line here skirts the banks of the River Wye and one of the pillars supporting the M48 Severn Bridge is visible in the background. **Jamie Squibbs**

Seeing Red : There can be little doubt this colour certainly brightens things up! On 14th February, the first Class 66/0 to be so applied - No.66152 (above) - passes Blackford with a train of loaded pipes for use in the North Sea gas/oil industry, running as 6S04, 05:52 (TO) Mossend - Raithes farm; the service originates as 6S04 from Hartlepool the day before, running to Mossend for staging overnight. The pipes are conveyed on purpose built 'BTA' bogie bolster pipe wagons. The train has passed the signal box, which controls this section of line, two sidings and the crossing barriers guarding the B8081 road. **Alastair Blackwood**

Class 67 No.67018 'Keith Heller' (below) looks impressive at the head of 1H53, the 15:55 Birmingham Moor Street - London Marylebone as it approaches Bordesley on 27th March - the background dominated by the offices and flats marking the commercial centre of Britain's second city, Birmingham. **David Weake**

Cumbrian Coasters

Ravenglass : Scafell, not to be confused with England's highest peak (Scafell Pike), looks gloomy in the background as DRS Class 20s Nos.20303 and 20304 (above) top 'n' tail three flasks over the River Mite viaduct at Ravenglass on 1st June with 6C52, (ThO) 16:05 Heysham - Sellafield.

This is the Lake District's only coastal village and where we see 6C52 again on 9th August at Mite viaduct, but this time with DRS Class 37/4s No.37423 'Spirit of the Lakes' and No.37419 'Lord Hinton' (below) running in top 'n' tail formation, which is the mode of operation for the Heysham flasks. At this point the rivers Mite, Irt and Esk all empty out into the Irish Sea.

Coulderton : Catching the setting sun's golden light, Nos.37419 'Lord Hinton' + No.37423 'Spirit of the Lakes' (above) accelerate away from St Bees on 8th August with 6M22, (WO) 12:17 Hunterston - Sellafield, seen here from the beach at Coulderton, with St Bees Head in the background.

Pow Beck Valley : Absolutely stunning scenery, with the Western Fells of Lakeland on the horizon - Grassmoor, above Crummock Water, on the left and Great Borne and Starling Dodd, in Ennerdale, to the centre and right. By the way, there's also Nos.37419 'Lord Hinton' + 37604 (below) scurrying through Pow Beck valley on 14th August, approaching the passing loop at St Bees station, on 6M60, (TO) 13:25 Seaton on Tees - Sellafield, consisting of two 'FNA' wagons, each housing a Magnox flask. **Eliot Andersen (4)**

Heritage Heavyweights Over Shap

Greenholme : What a super sight - a pair of DRS Class 37s working flat out on the ascent of Shap. On 11th September, DRS Class 37s (on hire to DBS) Nos.37608 +37609 (above) pass Greenholme with 4C03, 12:06 Washwood Heath - Carlisle formed of 'YXAs' carrying concrete sleepers. It is a shame additional stanchions have had to be erected here to spoil an otherwise fantastic setting. **Keith McGovern**

Making its first appearance on the logs from Carlisle, Colas Class 56 No.56094 (below) passes Greenholme on 22nd September heading in the opposite direction to the '37s' with 6J37, 12:44 Carlisle Yard - Chirk loaded timber wagons. The loco is picking up speed after being looped at Shap Summit. **Steven Brykajlo**

Tyne Valley Diverts

Gilsland : Anglo-Scottish East Coast diversions via the Tyne Valley take place on 15th September. As it dodges the shadows, No.67008 (above) tows No.91102 'City of York' and a full East Coast 225 set through Gilsland, while working the diverted 1E06, 06:50 Glasgow Central - London King's Cross service. This is the first time a 225 set is 'dragged' over the Tyne Valley line.

Great Corby : Later the same day, No.67008 (below) is now seen heading another East Coast 225 set (No.91103 on the rear) towards the foot crossing at Great Corby, this being the diverted 1S13, 11:00 London King's Cross - Edinburgh Waverley. **Steven Brykajlo (2)**

Four on the Firth of Forth

The Tide's in .... as DRS Class 66/4 No.66427 (above) skirts the River Forth at Culross on 29th September, while working the diverted 4A13, 12:20 Grangemouth - Craiginches Intermodal. The Stirling - Alloa - Kincardine link now allows trains to be routed this way and No.66427 will rejoin its normal route at Dundee. The turret of Dunimarle Castle can be seen poking its head above the tree line. **Jim Ramsay**

Heading in the opposite direction on 14th September, DBS Class 66/0 No.66140 (below) passes Culross with a vari-shaded rake of 'MEAs' forming 6G26, the 16:52 Earlseat - Hunterston service of blending coal. This is one of just two regular flows to run along the banks of the River Forth at Culross. **Guy Houston**

.... **and out** .... to record the other scheduled flow to run over this route; 6N72, 14:48 Linkswood - Grangemouth empty fuel oil tanks from RAF Leuchars. Colas Rail Class 66/8 No.66850 (above) heads west with 6N72 and a rake of 20 smart looking green 'TTA' 2-axle tanks, which work exclusively out of Grangemouth oil refinery to Lairg, Linkswood and Prestwick.   **Guy Houston**

Occasional trains of imported coal run from Leith Docks (Edinburgh) to Longannet power station, as on 1st July 2011, when FHH Class 66/5 No.66548 (below) passed Culross with the power station looming in the background with a rake of 'HHA' empties, running as 4Z04, the 09:11 Longannet - Leith via Dunfermline Townhill (reverse) and the Forth Bridge - four colourful images at a super location.   **Steven Brykajlo**

Multiple Aspects **Full House** in Eastleigh Yard on Saturday, 21st April, with every siding headed by a loco waiting the call for duty, most of which will be departmental 'trips' to various engineering possessions over the weekend. There are at least eight locos (above) visible, 1 × Class 60 (No.60039), 4 × Class 66/0s, 1 × Class 66/7 and 2 × Class 73s. **Simon Howard**

Perfect Symmetry as two FHH Class 66s (below) draw up alongside each other at Hatfield & Stainforth on 16th January with loaded coal hoppers, hauled by No.66545 and No.66953, respectively. Without any 'gen' on the day, train identification of such services is almost impossible! **Alan Padley**

Coming Home on 21st April: DBS Class 67 No.67029 is sent from Toton to collect 'shed' No.66016 from Longport following repair, plus Class 60s No.60043 and No.60092 from Crewe. All four locos (above) return to Toton and are passing Castle Donnington; Ratcliffe's cooling towers dominate. **Craig Adamson (2)**

Nemesis depot at Wetmore, Burton-on-Trent, was formerly a MGR wagon repair depot, but is now a busy place for loco hire and loco restoration, as can be seen in this view of four lines of locos (below), which are:

(l to r) : 56051 / 56065 / 56007 / 56117 / 56081 / 56060 / 09019 / 08389   45112 / 33012
            08892 / 56301 / 56302 / 37679 / 6515   47488 / 56018

Positioning Moves are commonplace, with locos included 'Dead In Tow' (DIT) in a scheduled service or in a multiple-loco light engine move in order to save on running costs. On 18th April, when 4N64, Doncaster - Tyne Dock passes Ranskelf, the photographer is treated to a bonus with three other '67/7s' (DIT) in the consist, destined for Tyneside and their next turn of duty. No.66734 'The Eco Express' (above) leads Nos.66728, 66736 and 66701, all of which except No.66701 are in GBRf / Europorte livery.   **Ian Ball**

Weekend 'Thameslink' Engineering work necessitates the use of all GBRF's active '73s' plus the hire of Nos.73109, 73136 and 73201. On 30th July, a seven-loco convoy passes Grove Park comprising No.73213 (below) leading Nos.73208, 66743, 73205, 73206, 73119 and 73212, running as 0X66, the 09:30 Eastleigh Yard - Tonbridge West Yard. Previously, light engine moves were restricted to a maximum of 5 locos coupled up, but this practice seems to have been extended to a maximum of 10-locos.   **Ian Cuthbertson**

On 26th July, DBS locos No.67026, 67029 and 66148 are hitching a ride as far as Wembley in the consist of 4O57, 14:20 Hams Hall - Dollands Moor intermodal. DBS Class 66/0 No.66030 (above) leads along the WCML, just south of Tring station. The '67s' are destined for London and will be used on additional passenger services laid on for the duration of the London 2012 Olympic Games. **Ian Cuthbertson**

DBS undertake **'92' Trials** to assess the suitability of a return to traffic for some stored Class 92s. Three '92s' are involved, each having a turn hauling the other two '92s' (DIT) + a rake of 'HTAs' between Carlisle and Warrington. On 12th July, No.92011 'Handel' (below) with No.92027 'George Eliot' + No.92025 'Oscar Wilde' pass Euxton Junction with 4Z62, the 15:45 Carlisle Yard - Warrington; Colas Class 66/8 No.66848 prepares to overtake with 6J37, 12:44 Carlisle Yard - Chirk loaded timber. **Fred Kerr**

"In The Heat Of The Night" : Under a clearing sky, five operational 'Deltics' (above / below) pose for the cameras during an organised photoshoot at Buckley Wells, East Lancs Railway, on 21st September and re-create a scene very reminiscent of Finsbury Park TMD. The locos are, from left to right:

55022 'Royal Scots Grey'
    55019 'Royal Highland Fusilier'
        55002 'King's Own Yorkshire Light Infantry'
            D9016 'Gordon Highlander'
                D9009 'Alycidon'

A photoshoot is very popular and gives enthusiasts the opportunity to hone their photographic skills, especially when it comes to getting the right exposure for nocturnal shots like these.   **Neil Harvey (2)**

Past and Present : Thorpe Marsh, Barnby Dun, on the Adwick Jct to Stainforth Jct 'freight only' line .

On 7th June 2011, Class 60 No.60071 'Ribblehead Viaduct' (above) passes the remnants of the defunct Thorpe Marsh power station - its cooling towers - while in charge of 6D49, 13:55 Ferrybridge - Lindsey fuel oil empties. Construction of the power station began in 1959 and was commissioned between 1963 and 1965, initially operated by the Central Electricity Generating Board followed by National Power after privatisation in 1990. The station closed in 1994.

Between April and August 2012, the original six cooling towers (each 340ft high and 260ft in diameter at the base) are pulled down; the first (south-westernmost) tower was demolished on 1st April, the north-easternmost on 10th June, the centre two on 5th August and the last two towers being pulled down on 19th August. This is the scene on 5th September, the cooling towers are no more and recently overhauled Class 60 No.60040 (below) passes the same spot with 6E32, 08:55 Preston Docks - Lindsey. **Alan Padley (2)**

The RHTT Season kicks off in October and locos and 'water canons' move into position to start work. In this striking shot, four DRS Class 57s Nos.57002, 57008, 57007 and 57003 (above) head away from the camera at Bessacarr (Doncaster) on 4th October en route to East Anglia, running as 6Z30, York - Stowmarket. The '57's and associated 'FEAs' will be based at Stowmarket, from where they will perform 'leaf-busting' duties in Norfolk, Suffolk and Essex.   **Alan Padley**

'Raising Steam'

"Over The Top at Wilpshire"

'Steam, glorious, Steam' .... as LMS Back 5, No.45305 (above) heralds the start of the next chapter as she reaches the summit of the climb from Blackburn on the approach to Ramsgreave & Wilpshire station on 20th August with 'The Mersey Moorlander' (1Z80, 06:06 Crewe - Carlisle) bound for the 'S. & C'.

On this line, there used to be a sand drag at Daiseyfield, at the foot of the gradient from Ramsgreave, which stems from the days when unfitted freights were diverted away from the electrified WCML to run via the Settle and Carlisle line. A runaway train could be re-directed via catch points into a sand drag to lessen the impact of a derailment.

As for this image, it couldn't have been much grimmer, but luckily 800ASA comes to the rescue! I really like this shot, the miserable conditions adding to the aesthetics and the photographer is to be applauded for his patience and resolve! When all said and done, the summer of 2012 will be remembered for what it wasn't - a summer!

Neil Harvey

'The Winter Cumbrian Mountain Express'

A combination of clear Cumbrian air, a freezing cold day and a double-header working flat out on a stiff climb are all essential ingredients to capture that magic moment, and so it was on Saturday, 28th January. LMS Class 5MT 4-6-0 'Black 5s' No.44871 and No.45407 'The Lancashire Fusilier' *(below)*, roar up Shap and shatter the peace in the process as they work a 'Winter Cumbrian Mountain Express', albeit displaying 'The Waverley' headboard - the train is running as 1Z67, the 07:48 Manchester Victoria - Carlisle.

Before & after .... the occasion is such a spectacle that an earlier shot captures the Black 5s *(top left)* storming through Tebay in the distance to begin the climb to Shap Summit; the smoke trail and constant roar from their exhaust signalling their imminent approach. Smoke hangs in the air *(above)* for well over half an hour as the aftermath of what has just taken place.

Finally, and as equally impressive, Nos.44871 and 45407 *(Page 182)* roar over Ais Gill summit with the return WCME (1Z68, 14:39 Carlisle - Manchester Victoria) at sunset on 28th January 2012. **Mark Walker (4)**

Castle Surmounts Ais Gill

'Shap, Settle & Carlisle'

Sometimes the unexpected is better than the planned outcome and, for many passengers, that's just what happens on Saturday, 10th March. A scheduled double-heading of LMS 4-6-2 No.6201 'Princess Elizabeth' + GWR Castle Class 4-6-0 No.5043 'Earl of Mount Edgcumbe' was supposed to work the 'Shap, Settle & Carlisle' charter over Shap and a return run over the Settle & Carlisle.

Unfortunately, the LMS Pacific loco fails at Carlisle with a warm tender hotbox and has to be left at Carlisle, leaving the Castle to run unassisted over the 'Long Drag' - load 11 and a 1 in 100 ruling gradient all the way from Appleby to Ais Gill.

Despite this, the 'Castle' puts in a sterling performance and manages to maintain timings for a double-headed train, actually gaining a minute by the time of the water stop at Hellifield.

With the 'Earl' running about 15 minutes early, the onlookers and photographers gathered at Ais Gill are blessed with sunshine, which disappears a couple of minutes later. No.5043 (Previous Page) is crossing Ais Gill viaduct on the final leg of the climb to the summit with 1Z91, 14:42 Carlisle - Tyseley return leg of the 'Shap, Settle & Carlisle' charter. As No.5043 did not have enough coal to go all the way back to Tyesely, the diesel which had brought the train to Carnforth in the morning, No.47500, is attached to the train at Warrington Bank Quay.

Alan Padley

The King Bows Out

On 17th March, Collett 4-6-0 No.6024 'King Edward 1' makes its last main line run heading a charter from Bristol to Kingswear, prior to temporary withdrawal for heavy overhaul at the West Somerset Railway's Minehead shed, reckoned to take two years to complete. The King's bottom end is to remain at Minehead whilst the boiler will be transported to Riley Engineering in Bury.

As a parting shot, here are a couple of images of the 'King' at work on its penultimate working on Saturday, 3rd March, heading the 'Bristolian' charter - 1Z26, 09:33 Bristol Temple Meads - London Paddington.

With a vey low early spring sun, the 'King' (opposite) dodges the shadows as it climbs the 1 in 100 'Dauntsey Bank' towards Royal Wootton Bassett - ten minutes later No.6024 (below) passes the former GWR general offices at Swindon, following an unscheduled stop. **Martin Buck** (opposite) **/ Steven King** (below)

GWR 5700 CLASS Fact File

Designer	:	Collett
Built	:	1929 - 1950
Built at	:	Swindon Works
		Armstrong Whitworth
		W. G. Bagnall
		Beyer, Peacock & Co.
		Kerr Stuart
		North British
		Yorkshire Engine Co.
Numbers	:	3600 - 3799
		4600 - 4699
		5700 - 5799
		6700 - 6779
		7700 - 7799
		8700 - 8799
		9600 - 9682
		9701 - 9799

The 'Double Lickey Banker'

On Saturday, 24th March, Bromsgrove is besieged by enthusiasts keen, not so much to witness the passing of LMS Princess Royal 4-6-2 Pacific No.6201 'Princess Elizabeth' but, to witness a much rarer event. The main attraction being No.6201 coming to a stand on 1Z65, 14:10 Bristol Temple Meads - Dorridge charter to attach a banker for the two mile assault of the famous 1 in 37 Lickey Incline. And that's not all - the banker is in the shape of Tyseley's GWR 0-6-0 Pannier Tanks No.7752 (running as No.L94) and No.9600 and are seen (above) making their way 'down' the Lickey in readiness for the challenge ahead.

No.6201 Princess Elizabeth (below) storms 'up' the steepest gradient in Britain towards Vigo Bridge, assisted at the rear by the two pannier tanks; the noise can only be described as volcanic and is the first time since 1964 that a train has been banked by two steam locos.   **Stephen Dance (2)**

Location	Time	
Tyseley Warwick Rd	07:55	
St Andrews Jct	08:09	
Castle Bromwich Jct	08:23	
Walsall	08:52	
Bescot 'Up Loop'	08:59 /	09:39
Aston	09:56	
Birmingham International	10:08 /	10:58
Aston	11:18	
Four Oaks	11:33	
Lichfield City	11:47 /	11:57
Alrewas	12:11 /	12:50
Moira	13:15	
Mantle Lane	13:35 /	14:13
Bardon Hill	14:18	
Knighton Jct	14:42 /	15:22
Hinckley	15:46	
Nuneaton	15:55	
Whitacre Jct	16:18 /	17:05
Water Orton	17:19	
St Andrews Jct	17:32	
Tyseley Warwick Rd	17:45	

East Midlands Rambling

Staying with a Pannier theme, on 14th April, Vintage Trains lay on the 'East Midlands Rambler' steam charter around the East Midlands featuring Tyseley's Pannier Tanks No.7752 (running as No.L94) and No.9600.

As a bonus, the tour takes in the following 'freight only' lines:

Sutton Park

Aston - Stechford

Burton - Coalville.

On the outward journey, Nos.L94 + No.9600 (above) are seen 'under the wires' at Shenstone on the Birmingham - Lichfield line with 1Z84, the 07:55 Tyseley Warwick Road - Mantle Lane - Tyseley Warwick Road charter.

On the return journey, Nos.L94 + 9600 (below) are seen again, this time passing Saltley, with the two well known gasometers dominating the skyline.   **David Weake (2)**

(Above) : On Day 5 of the 'GBV', 25th April, the two 'Black 5s', No.45305 + No.45407 'The Lancashire Fusilier' storm away from a speed restriction on the approach to Maybole before blasting through the station with 1Z80, Barnhill - Stranraer.   **Mark Walker**

The Great Britain V

The epic nine day Great Britain V steam charter (GBV) is celebrating its 5th anniversary - classic steam haulage throughout Great Britain - a mammoth undertaking indeed. For the first time, GBV deviates from its usual operation by splitting the train into two separate portions on day two, thus:

Portion One : Thornton Junction to Inverness (for the Kyle of Lochalsh)

Portion Two : Thornton Junction to Fort William (for Mallaig)

A sea ferry transfers passengers between Mallaig and the Kyle of Lochalsh, through the Sound of Sleat, so each set of passengers can enjoy the respective journeys - a convenient and enjoyable way of covering both lines. The two portions join up once again at Barnhill on Day 5 for the remainder of the tour.

To mark the fifth anniversary a small selection of images is included for your perusal along with a brief synopsis of the respective legs of the tour and the steam engines used.

Saturday, 21st April to Sunday, 29th April

Day 1	: London King's Cross - York	60019 'Bittern'	1Z20
	York - Edinburgh Waverley	70013 'Oliver Cromwell'	1Z20
Day 2	: Edinburgh Waverley - Thornton Junction	46115 'Scots Guardsman'	1Z28
	Thornton Junction - Inverness	46115 'Scots Guardsman'	1Z28
	Thornton Junction - Fort William	61994 'Great Marquess'	1Z29
Day 3	: Inverness - Kyle of Lochalsh - Inverness	45305	1Z34
	Kyle of Lochalsh - Inverness	45305	1Z35
	Fort William - Mallaig	61994 'Great Marquess'	1Z36
	Mallaig - Fort William	61994 'Great Marquess'	1Z37
Day 4	: Fort William - Ashfield	61994 'Great Marquess'	1Z66
	Inverness - Barnhill (Glasgow)	46115 'Scots Guardsman'	1Z38
Day 5	: Barnhill - Stranraer	45305 + 45407 'The Lancashire Fusilier'	1Z80
	Stranraer - Barnhill	45305 + 45407 'The Lancashire Fusilier'	1Z48
Day 6	: Barnhill - Carlisle - S & C - Preston	46233 'Duchess of Sutherland'	1Z34
Day 7	: Preston - Bristol Temple Meads	70013 'Oliver Cromwell'	1Z51
Day 8	: Bristol Temple Meads - Penzance	34067 'Tangmere' + 70013 'Oliver Cromwell'	1Z46
Day 9	: Bristol Temple Meads - London Paddington	5043 'Earl of Mount Edgcumbe'	1Z68

Leading up to GBV, the schedule of steam engines allocated to run does change right up to the last minute due to engine non-availability and operating constraints. For example, gauging issues prevent No.70013 'Oliver Cromwell' from running to Stranraer and the following steam engines were substituted beforehand:

No.60007 'Sir Nigel Gresley'   No.60163 'Tornado'

No. 5029 'Nunney Castle'   No. 6023 'King Edward II'

(Overleaf) :

(Page 190, top) : A contrast of styles .... A4 Pacific No.60019 'Bittern', running as LNER No.4464, is seen passing Tempsford, Bedfordshire, on the first leg of the 'GBV' railtour, 1Z20, 08:17 Kings Cross - Edinburgh. Class 91 No.91102 is punching a hole through the smoke as it passes on the 'Down Fast' line with 1S09, the 09:00 King's Cross - Edinburgh Waverley.   **Nigel Gibbs**

(Page 190, bottom) : Nos.45305 + 45407 attack the 1 in 67 gradient from Barrhill.   **Mark Walker**

(Page 191, top) : Meanwhile, in the south west of England, No.34067 'Tangmere' + No.70013 'Oliver Cromwell are hard at work as they pass Beam Bridge, near Wellington, on the ascent to Whiteball Summit with 1Z46, 08:15 Bristol Temple Meads - Penzance. It's day 8 and the penultimate steam leg of 'GBV '.

(Page 191, bottom) : A close up shot of No.34067 as it leads 1Z46 along the River Exe estuary at Powderham, near Starcross, en route to Penzance.   **Peter Slater (2)**

'GBV' - a final offering .... and two great shots to boot! No.46115 'Scots Guardsman' (above) is racing an impending storm as it literally storms south at Kinbuck, Dunblane, on the Perth - Glasgow main line in splendid light on the eve of 24th April with 1Z38, Inverness - Barnhill leg of the 'GBV'.

Meanwhile, on the former Glasgow & South Western Main Line, No.46233 'Duchess of Sutherland' (below) races through New Cumnock with 'GBV' on 26th April (day 6), running as 1Z34, Barnhill - Preston. The train is passing the 1907 built signal box, which has recently been refurbished, and is operational 24 hours a day. Note also, No.46233 is now sporting Brunswick green livery.

Mark Walker (2)

The Cathedrals Explorer

The appetite for steam seems to be insatiable, every weekend with Wednesdays and Thursdays thrown in for good measure during spring and summer. As if one nine-day epic is not enough, Steam Dreams come up with their own version, just under three weeks after the completion of 'GBV' organised by the Railway Touring Company.

Friday, 18th May to Friday, 25th May

Date		Route	Locomotive	Headcode
18th	:	Staines - London Victoria	70000 'Britannia'	1Z10
		London Victoria - Durham	60163 'Tornado'	1Z11
19th	:	Durham - Perth	60019 'Bittern'	1Z22
		Perth - Inverness	60163 'Tornado'	1Z24
20th	:	Inverness - Kyle of Lochalsh	61994 'Great Marquess'	1Z31
		Kyle of Lochalsh - Inverness	61994 'Great Marquess'	1Z32
22nd	:	Inverness - Aberdeen	60163 'Tornado'	1Z35
		Aberdeen - Edinburgh Waverley	60163 'Tornado'	1Z37
23rd	:	Edinburgh Waverley - Edinburgh Waverley	60019 'Bittern'	1Z42
24th	:	Edinburgh Waverley - Carlisle	60019 'Bittern'	1Z43
		Carlisle - Hellifield	60019 'Bittern'	1Z44
25th		Hellifield - London Victoria	46201 'Princess Elizabeth'	1Z76

(above) : A1 Pacific, No.60163 'Tornado' is seen skirting the Angus Coast at Boddin Point with 1Z37, the 17:42 Aberdeen - Edinburgh leg of 'The Cathedrals Explorer' on 22nd May. **Jim Ramsay**

(Opposite) :

(top right) : As the sun begins to dip below the fells, No.60019 'Bittern', running under the guise of No.4464 in LNER garter blue livery, looks stunning as she whisks the homeward bound 'Cathedrals Explorer' through Dentdale and over Arten Gill Viaduct. **Mark Walker**

(bottom right) : Meanwhile, No.46201 (6201) 'Princess Elizabeth' passes Ashwell, County Rutland, on the Melton Mowbray - Oakham main line with 1Z76, the 11:11 Hellifield - London Victoria. This long stretch of the tour was routed via Skipton, Chesterfield, Toton, Syston North Junction, Corby, Bedford, Acton Wells Junction, Barnes and Clapham Junction. **Nigel Gibbs**

'Derek Holmes' Assists

This particular 'Cathedrals Express' was originally advertised to run on 2nd July 2011 hauled by 4-6-2 Pacific No.60019 'Bittern' and Class 8f 2-8-0 No.48151, but finally runs on 10th March with No.60163 'Tornado' from Paddington to Plymouth. However, assistance in the shape of DBS Class 66 No.66152 'Derek Holmes Railway Operator' is required over the Devon banks between Exeter and Plymouth.

'Tornado' and No.66152 (above) are first seen at Powderham with 1Z29, the 08:06 London Paddington - Plymouth 'Cathedrals Express' running alongside the River Exe estuary. On the return journey, a more panoramic shot sees No.60163 + 66152 (below) passing Combefishacre with 1Z30, 17:05 Plymouth - London Paddington working flat out on the ruling 1 in 45 climb to Dainton Summit. **Peter Slater / Robert Sherwood**

Duchess Goes Green

On 3rd March, LMS Princess Coronation Class 4-6-2 Pacific No.46233 'Duchess of Sutherland' is rolled out in authentic green livery at the Midland Railway Centre, Butterley, following overhaul.

No.46233 was outshopped (as No.6233) in July 1938 from Crewe Works, part of the third batch of her class. These engines were unstreamlined, painted in LMS standard crimson lake livery and had a single chimney and no smoke deflectors.

She was initially allocated to Camden (London), acquiring a double chimney in March 1941 and smoke deflectors in September 1945, prior to being painted in postwar LMS black livery in September 1946. With the creation of British Railways in January 1948, she was allocated to Crewe North depot and given her BR number 46233 in October 1948, being finally repainted in BR Brunswick green livery in the early 1950's. In June 1958 she was allocated to Carlisle Upperby before being withdrawn from Edge Hill depot in February 1964.

Following withdrawal, she was acquired by Butlins 'Heads-of-Ayr' holiday camp in October 1964 and later moved to Bressingham Steam Museum, Diss (Norfolk). She was subsequently acquired by The Princess Royal Class Locomotive Trust and fully restored to working order at the Midland Railway Centre at a cost of over £350,000. To allow mainline running, she has been fitted with Train Protection & Warning System (TPWS), On-Train Monitoring Recorder (OTMR) and Automatic Warning System (AWS).

On 21st April, No.46233 'Duchess of Sutherland' (below) cruises through Kilnhurst while at the head of 'The Yorkshire Coronation'; 1Z82, the 07:55 Derby - Scarborough. The driver had sighted an adverse signal, hence the exhaust just starting to collapse.   **Neil Harvey**

'Popex'

May 1982

30 Years ago, in the summer of 1982, His Holiness Pope John Paul II travelled to Great Britain for a historic six day tour that saw him greet and bless hundreds of thousands of people at 16 different venues. It was the first time a pope had visited Great Britain in over 400 years.

It's not that 'Loco Review' is getting all religious, but this papal visit generated unprecedented levels of loco hauled activity with relief trains (**'Popex'**) and local DMU services going over to loco and coaches to cater for the anticipated passengers attending the open air masses.

The Pope's visit to Heaton Park, Manchester, on Monday, 31st May 1982, was specially worthy of attention as the majority of DMU services on the Manchester Victoria - Preston - Blackpool North route would be loco hauled, most diagrammed for Class 40 traction - I decided to sample the traction on offer and this is my log of the day's proceedings:

Haulage

Loco	Journey made	Mileage	Train Reporting Details
40027	Llandudno Jct - Manchester V	84.50	2J62, 01:18 Llandudno Jct - Manchester V
40129	Manchester V - Preston	30.75	2P64, 09:15 Manchester V - Blackpool N
40020	Preston - Manchester V	30.75	2J64, 09:40 Blackpool N - Manchester V
40094	Manchester V - Blackpool N	48.25	2P64, 12:45 Manchester V - Blackpool N
25189	Blackpool N - Kirkham	9.75	2J64, 14:10 Blackpool N - Manchester V
40162	Kirkham - Blackpool N	9.75	2P64, 13:15 Manchester V - Blackpool N
40094	Blackpool N - Manchester V	48.25	2J64, 15:15 Blackpool N - Manchester V
40183	Manchester V - Preston	30.75	2P64, 16:45 Manchester V - Blackpool N
40020	Preston - Manchester V	30.75	2J64, 17:10 Blackpool N - Manchester V
40022	Manchester V - Kirkham	38.50	2P64, 18:45 Manchester V - Blackpool N
40094	Kirkham - Manchester V	38.50	2J64, 20:10 Blackpool N - Manchester V
40192	Manchester V - Preston	30.75	2P64, 22:10 Manchester V - Blackpool N

(Above) : Class 40 No.40027 'Parthia' acts as 'Thunderbird' at Manchester Victoria on 31st May 1982.

Class 40 No.40092 has a busy few days over the Spring Bank Holiday (29th to 31st May 1982), starting on Saturday morning (29th) by working 2J64, the 06:50 Blackpool North - Manchester Victoria. No.40092 (above) awaits departure with 2J64 with the famous Blackpool Tower dominating the skyline. Upon arrival at Manchester, No.40092 and stock form 1E19, the 08:40 service to Scarborough and 1M69, 12:00 return.

On Sunday (30th), No.40092 takes an ECS to Barrow in Furness in readiness for a 22:45hrs 'Popex' to Bolton - thence, onto the 2J64 / 2P64 diagram the following day. **Martin Buck (2)**

Class 40 Turns - Monday, 31st May 1982 : Manchester - Blackpool

40001	2P64, 15:45 MV - BN	2J64, 18:10 BN - MV	2P64, 21:15 MV - BN
40020	2J64, 09:40 BN - MV	2P64, 14:45 MV - BN	2J64, 17:10 BN - MV
	2P64, 20:15 MV - BN		
40022	2J64, 08:40 BN - MV	2P64, 12:15 MV - BN	2J64, 14:40 BN - MV
	2P64, 18:45 MV - BN	2J64, 21:10 BN - MV	
40027	2J62, 01:18 LJ - MV	('Thunderbird' at MV)	
40052	2J64, 08:10 BN - MV	(Ran out of fuel at Preston)	
40069	2J64, 06:10 BN - MV	2P64, 09:45 MV - BN	2J64, 12:10 BN - MV
40077	2J64, 04:00 BN - MV	2P64, 08:45 MV - BN	2J64, 11:10 BN - MV
	2P64, 14:15 MV - BN	2J64, 16:40 BN - MV	2P64, 19:45 MV - BN
	2J64, 22:10 BN - MV		
40092	2J64, 06:40 BN - MV	2P64, 11:15 MV - BN	2J64, 13:40 BN - MV
	2P64, 19:15 MV - BN	2J64, 21:40 BN - MV	
40094	2J64, 09:10 BN - MV	2P64, 12:45 MV - BN	2J64, 15:10 BN - MV
	2P64, 17:45 MV - BN	2J64, 20:10 BN - MV	
40129	2P64, 09;15 MV - BN	2J64, 11:40 BN - MV	
40162	2J64, 10:10 BN - MV	(47349 failed on departure) 2P64, 13:15 MV - BN	
	2J64, 15:40 BN - MV		
40183	2J64, 07:10 BN - MV	(47485 fails / 40162 'pushes' from Chorley to Bolton / 40162 to MV	
	2P64, 10:15 MV - BN	2J64, 12:40 BN - MV 2P64, 16:45 MV - BN	
40192	2J64, 19:10 BN - MV	2P64, 22:10 MV - BN	

Selective Images :

(Top Left) : 502 'Flying Scotsman'

Whilst still undergoing overhaul, the famous A3 Pacific No.502 'Flying Scotsman' arrives from the East Lancashire Railway (Bury) to go on display at 'Railfest'.

She is minus con rods, sports the interim number 502 (usually No.4472) and is turned out in drab wartime black livery.

While at York, work will be carried out on pipework, valve gear and lubrication system. **Mark Walker**

(Below) :

46229 'Duchess of Hamilton'

This 'Duchess' was built in 1938 at Crewe as the tenth member of its class, the last in the second batch of five red streamliners, complete with gold 'speed cheat' stripes.

In September 2005, the NRM announced that No.46229 would return to its original streamlined appearance. The work was carried out at Tyseley Locomotive Works and in May 2009 she returned to the NRM, going on display in an exhibition called "Duchess of Hamilton Streamlined: 'Styling An Era'. She certainly looks good!

Nigel Gibbs (3)

(Top Right) : 56312

The 'Flagship' loco and mobile advertiser for 'Railfest'. No.56312 stands alongside one of DRS' recently acquired Class 57/3s, No.57309.

(Below) : 57309

Since completion of the West Coast Main Line upgrade work, Virgin's requirement for '57s' decreases and the '57/3' fleet is finding new homes.

Nos.57302 and 57304, plus No.57309 'Pride of Crewe' have been transferred to DRS; the latter posing for the cameras in new DRS colours and branding.

'RAILFEST'

'Railfest' takes place at the National Railway Museum, (NRM) during 2nd - 10th June and more than 33,000 people visit the event, with another 30,000 visiting the museum only.

It features a wide array of modern traction exhibits, many of which are record holders or pioneers of their class. As well as the first-built examples of the Class 20s, 37s, and 40s, there are also three variants of Class 57 that play such a diverse role on today's railways.

On 30th May, Class 60 No.60015, fresh out of the paint shop following overhaul at Toton, travels to York for the display bringing Class 395 'Javelin' unit No.395019 from Dollands Moor to the show. This, combined with several famous steam engines like 'Tornado', 'Flying Scotsman' and streamlined 'Duchess of Hamilton in LMS maroon livery, for example, provide great diversity for the visitors - in fact, something for everyone.

ABP Immingham

100 Years

The Port of Immingham was opened by King George V on 22nd July 1912 and celebrates its **Centenary** in 2012. Apparently, the King was so impressed with the Port and its facilities, he borrowed a sword and knighted the General Manager, Sir Sam Fay, there and then!

To commemorate the occasion, GBRf name Class 66/7 No.66742 'Port of Immingham' at the Humber Import terminal on 27th April, attended by GBRf MD John Smith, Port Director John Fitzgerald and Michael Portillo.

Immingham is now the busiest Associated British Port with over 50 million tonnes handled each year and around 25% of British railfreight originates here. Up to 250 trains a week leave the port, mostly imported coal and iron ore, plus petroleum products from the Humber and Lindsey refineries.

A Community Open Day is held on 22 July 2012, exactly 100 years to the day after its opening, so the public can see vessels and other exhibits and operations.

(Above) : Recently overhauled Class 60 No.60019 'Port of Grimsby and Immingham' poses for the cameras at the Port's Community Open Day along with a 'BYA' covered steel carrier, biomass hopper and a 'HTA' coal hopper, all of which are resplendent in DBS corporate red. **Alan Padley**

(Top) : Nameplate bestowed on No.66742 - 'Port of Immingham Centenary 1912 - 2012'. **Carl Gorse**

No.66020 (above) is seen snaking across Humber Road Junction and entering Immingham Reception Sidings with 6E80, 15:30 Wolverhampton Steel Terminal - Immingham Nordic Terminal empty 'BYA' steel coil carriers. These will be loaded overnight with imported steel coil from the Baltic countries and again transported to West Midlands for distribution across the Midlands. Humber Road Junction is the main access point for coal, ore and steel trains running to and from the docks. Humber oil refinery is on the left protruding above the tree-line. **Grant Mitchell**

The newly named Class 667/7 No.66742 'Port of Immingham' (below) crosses the River Dun navigation on 29th May with a loaded coal train, running as 6C18, Immingham - Eggborough. Some of the cooling towers of the defunct Thorpe Marsh power station loom large above the railway. **Alan Padley**

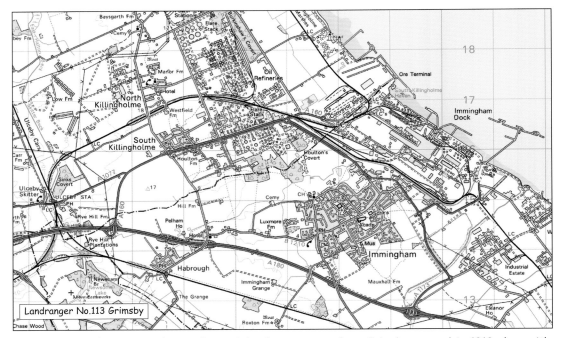

Landranger No.113 Grimsby

Immingham Docks : Immingham is located 6 miles upstream from Grimsby, opened in 1912 along with Immingham depot, by the Great Central Railway. It is now the UK's largest port by tonnage and handles more associated train movements than any other UK port. Its principle commodities are imported coal, iron ore and petrochemicals. **Courtesy Ordnance Survey mapping @ Crown Copyright Media 035/12**

Coal : By far the largest number of train movements (about 50%) involve imported coal with trainloads despatched by DBS, Freightliner Heavy Haul and GBRf to English power stations, mostly to Drax and Eggborough. In Arctic conditions , No.66133 (below) waits to depart from Immingham HIT Terminal on 10th February with 6H41, the 22:45 loaded coal departure to Drax Power Station. No wonder the driver looks on in anticipation, the train is running five hours late due to the freezing weather! **Nathan Seddon**

The night shift begins .... No.66090 (above) is seen on the former NCB No1 Coal Pad at Immingham loading its 21 HTA hoppers that will take around 1,900 tons of coal to Drax Power Station once loaded. The train's reporting details are 6H57, the 00:40 Immingham NCB1 - Drax.

FHH Class 66/5 No.66555 (below) is waiting for its crew to turn up and crank the loco back into life ready for another weeks work! Having being loaded on the Saturday evening the train is fully loaded with coal and, once the train has been made fit for service, it will depart as 6F49, the 21:30 service to Cottam power station. In the distance, FHH No.66552 can be seen having done the same, being parked up over the weekend having its train loaded for a service to Eggborough power Station. A set of GBRF 'HYA' / 'IIAs' can also be seen waiting its loco to arrive. **Grant Mitchell (2)**

'JAs' at 50

The Class 73 is an electro-diesel locomotive and is unusual in that it can operate from a 750 V DC third-rail or an on-board diesel engine to allow it to operate on non-electrified routes. This makes it very versatile, although the diesel engine produces less power than is available from the third-rail supply; for this reason these locos tended not to stray from the former Southern Region of British Rail.

The first six locos were built by BR at Eastleigh works in 1962 and were numbered E6001-E6006 and classified as type 'JA'. With the introduction of TOPS in 1968 they were to have been classified as Class 72 but instead became Class 73/0.

In the early 1970's the loco were renumbered 73001 - 73006.

The narrow box-like body allowed use all over the Southern Region network, including through the narrow tunnels on the Hastings Line and, being equipped for multiple working, could work with other locos and many Southern Region EMUs / DEMUs in push-pull train operation.

Merseyrail Electrics secured a fleet of four Class 73/0 locos (Nos. 73001, 73002, 73004*, 73005 and 73006), based at Birkenhead North TMD, for use on shunting and other departmental duties. Two, Nos.73001 and 73006 were repainted into Merseyrail's yellow livery. They were later fitted with sandite discharging equipment and reclassified as Class 73/9 and all four locos were withdrawn from traffic by 2002.

*No.73004 was used for spare parts and was the first to be cut up.

All five 'JAs' survived into preservation:

Numbers	Final Livery	Operator	Withdrawn	Status
E6001				
73001				
73901	Merseyrail	Merseyrail	05/2000	Preserved
E6002				
73002	BR Blue Large Logo	Merseyrail	11/1995	Preserved
E6003				
73003	BR Green	EWS	09/1996	Preserved
E6004				
73004	Bluebell Railway Blue	British Rail	09/1991	Scrapped
E6005				
73005	BR Blue	Merseyrail	12/2001	Preserved
E6006				
73006				
73906	Merseyrail	Merseyrail	12/2001	Preserved

The Class 73 fleet numbered 49 in total and the remaining 43 locomotives were built by Vulcan Foundry between 1965 and 1967. They were classified 'JB' and numbered E6007 - E6049, differing slightly from the 'JAs' in having an increased tractive effort and a higher maximum speed of 90 mph (80mph for the 'JAs'). Under TOPS, these became Class 73/1 and numbered 73101 - 73142. One loco, No.E6027, had already been withdrawn following accident damage and so was not renumbered.

73001

Southern Region motive power on parade. A relatively clean line-up at Hither Green diesel depot in South London comprises 'ED' No.73001 (above) and two Class 33s, No.33209 and No.33053. The narrow body of No.33209 built to Hastings line gauge is clearly evident. The photograph was taken on 20th March 1976, when permission to wander around a BR diesel depot was more freely given. **David Hayes**

No.73001 (below) ended its working life on Merseyside and is seen here circa. 1999 stabled alongside No.73002 (in BR Blue Large Logo livery) on Birkenhead North shed, looking rather smart in Merseyrail yellow livery with a grey band running along the bottom of the body side. **Ian Cuthbertson Collection**

'JA' Parade

Selective Images :

(Above) : **E6001**

Lydney Junction road crossing.

Beautifully restored in original green livery, this operational 'JA' is based at the Dean Forest Railway, which was formed in 1970 to preserve the Lydney to Parkend branch line.

(Centre) : **73002**

Stabled at Norwood Junction.

Stored as surplus to requirements and used as spares at Kirkdale with No.73005. Now preserved as a static display at Lydney and used for spares and storage. It is heavily stripped, but retains the power unit from No.73132.

(Bottom Left) : **E6003**

Ropley.

This view shows No.E6003 (73003) in its original livery, having been restored to 1960's green livery by Selhurst TMD for the last few months of its BR life.

(Top Right) : 73004

No. 73004 poses at Eastleigh for a night shot on 18th February 1978. The driver kindly turned on the cab light and stood still for the 20 odd second exposure. The DEMU behind is a Class 205 3-car Hampshire unit No.1128.

No.73004 did not survive the cutter's torch and was scrapped at Kingsbury by HNRC in February 2004 - used as a source of spares for No.73003.   **David Hayes**

(Centre) : 73005

Stabled at Norwood Junction.

This loco is owned by the Dean Forest Railway and is now a static display.

The front end of the 'JAs' differ from the other 'EDs' by having an additional jumper on the driver's side.

(Below) : 73006

Eastleigh

The former Merseyrail Class 73 was returned to BR Blue livery and appeared at Eastleigh in May 2009 as part of the celebrations to mark Eastleigh Works centenary.

Simon Howard (5)

50026 'Indomitable'

Background

No.50026 'Indomitable' worked its last train in November 1990 and was withdrawn a month later due to power unit damage, becoming the 25th Class 50 loco to be withdrawn after a working life of more than 22 years; amassing a total of 8,039 engine hours.

In early 1992, it was sent in a batch of nine locos to Booths scrap yard in Rotherham along with Nos.50001 / 004 / 016 / 020 / 023 / 026 / 036 / 040 and 045. All these formed part of a bid by 'Operation Collingwood' but, due to financial constraints and, to cut a long story short, only No.50026 was secured.

'Operation Collingwood' was a charity formed to train young engineering apprentices by getting them to rebuild railway locos. Class 50s were chosen as they were a British design.

Preservation Timeline

January 1992 - April 1993

Booths Scrapyard

15th April 1993

Class 47 No.47332 tows No.50026 to the Mid Hants Railway.

17th October 1994

No.50026 towed to Arncott, MoD Bicester by Class 37 No.37219.

Arrival at Bicester meant that restoration could now start on what was, effectively, a wreck due to years of vandalism and parts robbery whilst at Tavistock Yard (Plymouth) and at Booths. The assessment was a complete rebuild, overhaul, replacement of all components and rewiring.

The inside of the loco was shot blasted and re-sprayed making the loco 'as new'.

23rd March 2002

Major components returned to the loco - vacuum exhausters, traction motor blowers, radiator fan and motor and brake frame.

December 2003

Bogies off No.50001 'Dreadnought' delivered to Bicester for use on No.50026 - 'Dreadnought' scrapped in December 2002 after 11 years spent at Booths scrapyard.

13th April 2007

Loco moves to a new site within the Bicester MoD complex.

13th July 2005

Loco moves to Railway Vehicle Engineering Ltd (RVEL), Derby, by road.

9th April 2009

No.50026 is started up for the first time in 18 years at Old Oak Common.

17th April 2009

Class 47 No.47580 hauls No.50026 and No.50035 to Eastleigh Works for further restoration work and display at Eastleigh Works Centenary weekend.

11th May 2012

Following one of the most expensive and protracted loco restoration projects, No.50026 'Indomitable' makes the long-awaited comeback at the Swanage Railway gala.

50026 'Indomitable'

Amidst two fine examples of Southern semaphore 'pegs', No.50026 (above) comes off the single line into Corfe Castle on Sunday, 13th May, with the 14:30, Norden - Swanage. This is a real treat for 'Hoover' enthusiasts to witness the loco's first working in more than 22 years!   **Robert Sherwood**

At the end of May (25th - 27th) No.50026 becomes the star attraction at the Keighley & Worth Valley Railway's diesel gala, albeit with mixed fortunes! Despite its failure on the Friday and again on Saturday morning, sterling work was put in to ensure No.50026 makes two round trips late afternoon on Saturday and all the 'booked' turns on Sunday. No.50026 (below) is seen here on 27th May playing to the crowds, as it climbs the bank at Oakworth with the 13:17 Keighley - Oxenhope.   **Nathan Seddon**

26038

The Return

Class 26 No.26038 hauls its first train since withdrawal by British Rail in October 1992 when it makes its long-awaited passenger debut on 6th May.

It is a modest return, running just under a mile on the Barry Tourist Railway from Barry Hood Road to Barry island with three ex-Gatwick Express coaches in tow and Eurostar liveried and Dellner coupling fitted Class 73 No.73118 at the rear. The loco's looking resplendent in BR Blue livery, full yellow ends and fitted with snow-ploughs.

Loco History

In Traffic

Entered service on 28th August 1959 / withdrawn on 19th October 1992.

Numbers

D5338 - renumbered 26038 on 27th July 1974.

Depot Allocations

Haymarket (64B)	August 1959
Inverness (60A)	February 1960
Haymarket (HA)	September 1986
Eastfield (ED)	May 1987
Inverness (IS)	August 1992

Liveries

Originally in green livery, plus small yellow warning panel, followed by BR Blue in the 1970's.

May 1986 : Railfreight Grey with yellow cabs, black cab window surrounds and red solebars.

February 1992 : Dutch ('Civil Link') grey with yellow upper body sides and lower cab fronts and black window surrounds.

Notes :

a) No.26038 spent 26yrs and 8mths at Inverness - the longest allocation of all the '26s'.

b) May 1986 - last overhaul, air brakes fitted and boiler and water tanks removed.

c) 9th November 1985 - Last Class 26 to work the Far North Line, piloting No.37263 on the evening 17:15hrs Inverness - Wick service.

d) 14th October 1992 - Last working - AR14, 23:00 Barassie - Glengarnock ballast trip. No.26038 declared a failure with traction motor defect - assigned inspection at Inverness.

e) 16th October 1992 - Loco reaches Inverness (DIT) via 6Z33, Millerhill - Inverness.

f) 19th October 1992 - No.26038 withdrawn.

Preservation

a) September 1993 - No.26038 purchased for preservation.

b) December 1994 - loco moved by road to South Yorkshire Railway at Meadowhall.

c) January 2001 - loco purchased by Tom Clift and moves to Cardiff Cathays depot for overhaul, under the auspices of Pullman Ltd.

d) 17th June 2005 - No.26038 leaves Cardiff Cathays (to be demolished) for Cardiff Canton, via temporary storage at MoD Ashchurch, where restoration will be completed.

e) 28th March 2012 - restoration complete, Class 56 No.56312 tows No.26038 to Barry.

26038

On 6th May, BRCW Class 26 No.26038 (above) remarkably hauls a train for the first time in 20 years, when the snow-plough fitted Scottish loco hauls the first service of the day on the Barry Tourist Railway. It is seen on the Causeway as it approaches Barry Island with three Gatwick Express coaches and Class 73 No.73118 at the rear. **Jamie Squibbs**

The former Inverness machine makes a welcome return North of the Border on 27th July when it attends the SRPS diesel gala at the Bo'ness & Kinneil Railway. No.26038 (below) is seen on display at the rear of the 20:30hrs service from Manuel Junction, upon arrival at Bo'ness, as the late evening sun starts to set. There are two resident Class 26s based at Bo'ness, No.26004 and No.26024, both owned by 6LDA. **Jim Ramsay**

The 'Westerns' Golden Jubilee

Overview : Whilst the prototype Class 52 No.D1000 'Western Enterprise' was outshopped from Swindon Workshops in December 1961, the majority (in fact the remaining 73 members of the class) did not start to roll off the production line in earnest until 1962 onwards. The Class effectively celebrating a 'Golden Jubilee' in four consecutive years.

When switching to diesel traction as part of the 1950s Modernisation Plan, BR designed (and commissioned designs) for a large number of locomotive types. At this time, BR's regions had a high degree of autonomy, which extended as far as classes of locomotives ordered. Whilst almost all other diesel locomotives were diesel-electric, the Western Region employed a policy of using diesel-hydraulic traction - which would ultimately be their downfall.

Build :

D1001 - D1014	Swindon	1962	D1015 - D1026	Swindon	1963
D1027 - D1029	Swindon	1964	D1030 - D1032	Crewe	1963
D1033 - D1034	Crewe	1964	D1035 - D1046	Crewe	1962
D1047	Crewe	1963	D1048 - D1049	Crewe	1962
D1050 - D1073	Crewe	1963			

Allocation : Initially, the Class was allocated to Bath Road (Bristol), Canton (Cardiff), Laira (Plymouth), Landore (Swansea) and Old Oak Common (London). However, as the majority of passenger expresses worked to & from Paddington, the stretch of GWML between Reading and London saw the greatest intensity of 'Westerns'.

Names : While the first 'Western' was being constructed, proposals for livery and names were prepared by the BR design panel. They were to be named after famous West of England place names but, in the end, the Class were named with heraldic and regimental terms, prefixed with the word 'Western'. So, the 'D1000s' became known as 'Westerns'.

Dawlish Warren : *Making the most of her final 3 weeks of life on BR, Class 52 No. 1021 'Western Cavalier' (above) looks and sounds in great shape as she hauls an 'Up' express through Dawlish Warren in the late afternoon of 23rd July 1976.*

Westbury Station : No.D1049 'Western Monarch' (above) rolls into Westbury station under the much admired semaphores on the afternoon of 17th July 1975 with an unidentified West of England express. This happened to be the photographer's favourite Western Region station, coming closest to bridging the gap between the nostalgia of steam and the diesel era.

Colour light signalling (MAS) had reached Westbury by September 1978, where construction of a new signalling centre had started in 1981. However, it was not until March 1987 that Westbury finally linked up with Exeter signalling centre, when Taunton East signal box was taken out of use.

The End : BR Headquarters in Marylebone (London) produced a 'National Traction Plan' in 1967 which decreed that diesel-hydraulic locos would be phased out. This decision was not entirely unreasonable as the 'Westerns' did not have Electrical Train Supply (ETH) and some had only vacuum brakes, so preventing them from working air-conditioned passenger stock. This, combined with the fact Class 50s were needing a new home following electrification of the WCML, made the 'Westerns' ideal candidates for withdrawal and the '50s' migrated south.

The first Class 52s to be withdrawn were Nos.D1019 'Western Challenger' and D1032 'Western Marksman', which were taken out of service in May 1973 and by February 1977 the entire Class had gone. The final day of the 'Westerns' came on 26th February 1977 when the Western Region organised a triangular main line tour entitled the 'Western Tribute', running:

        (1st leg) : Paddington - Swansea
        (2nd leg) : Swansea   - Plymouth
        (3rd leg) : Plymouth   - Paddington

The charter was double-headed by Nos.D1013 'Western Ranger' and D1023 'Western Fusilier' with 650 passengers aboard and thousands more turning out on the day.

Preservation : It is a great shame the prototype desert-sand liveried No.D1000 'Western Enterprise' was not preserved but, fortunately, seven Class 52s, survived the cutter's torch:

        D1010 'Western Campaigner'   D1013 'Western Ranger'
        D1015 'Western Champion'   D1023 'Western Fusilier'
        D1041 'Western Prince'   D1048 'Western Lady'
        D1062 'Western Courier'

Photography : Images for this special portfolio kindly contributed by **David Hayes** (Frodsham).

Exeter St. Davids :

In and around Exeter, the area was blessed with some splendid examples of GWR lower quadrant semaphores, as illustrated here.

In a typical early summer morning scene in the 1970s, No.1025 'Western Guardsman' (top left) is standing in the 'Down' platform at St. David's station on 1st July 1974 with 1B03, the 07.30 Paddington - Penzance.

Note, the three car DMU set No.P358 waiting to leave for Exmouth.

On 24th July 1976, No.D1072 'Western Glory' (opposite) stands at Exeter St. David's awaiting 'the off' with a rake of 'Siphon Gs'. The original GWR Siphon G was a wooden, enclosed, milk churn transport wagon, built specifically as the GWR served a rural and highly agricultural West of England and South Wales.

After milk started to go by road, the early Siphons were withdrawn and the later dual-bogie versions used to transport parcels, some were often used by the engineer's department (with 'ENPARTS' in large letters on the side) to transport spares around the network.

Exeter Riverside : A lucky grab shot from a passing train catches No.D1063 'Western Monitor' (above) at Exeter Riverside Yard having arrived on 18th July 1975 with 6V53, the 04.24 Stoke Cockshute Yard - St. Blazey china clay empties. It is interesting that a Class 08 shunter is on the other end - possibly removing a faulty wagon, or wagons destined for somewhere else; the guard strolling across the tracks with the paperwork, the driver and second man sitting patiently in the cab for the off, 'vanfits' in the yard, the signal box, all reminiscent of those halcyon days in the 1970's - ah, nostalgia indeed!

Teignmouth : This is the view from the end of the photographer's road in 1976 ..... Alexandra Terrace, Teignmouth. Here, No.D1005 'Western Venturer' (above) is seen passing, heading west with what is believed to be 1B73, the 14;30 Paddington - Paignton. In the final few years, it became common practice for the loco number to be displayed in the headcode panel, although I am sure many would have preferred to see the correct train reporting code displayed to aid train recognition!

Aller Junction : On 22nd July 1976, No.D1065 'Western Consort' (below) is signalled for the Plymouth line at Aller Junction and prepares for the ascent of Dainton, an arduous and ruling gradient of 1 in 44 . Although looking a little worse for wear, No.1065 is still up to tackling the challenging south Devon banks (Whiteball, Dainton and Hemerden) on a Class 1 Express with little more than 3 months to go before withdrawal.

Newton Abbot : Sunday Best...... No.D1010 'Western Campaigner' (above) arrives at Newton Abbot with 1A39, the 13;30 Paignton - Paddington on 30th June 1974; the fashions of the day clearly evident for all to see.

(Overleaf) :

Bodmin Road : Few trains carry the romance of the 'Cornish Riviera Ltd' and even in the diesel days its imminent arrival still brought a tingle of anticipation - especially knowing it was likely to be hauled by a 'Western', the 14th July 1975 was no exception .... No.D1009 'Western Invader' (page 220) pauses at Bodmin Road (now Bodmin Parkway) with the 'Up' morning working.

Truro : Taken from a train approaching Truro station, a lucky shot catches No.D1040 'Western Queen' (page 221) shunting wagons in the station yard on 16th July 1975, which include some Presflo wagons bound for the Blue Circle cement terminal at Chacewater.

Plymouth : Destined for preservation, 'Western' No. D1048 'Western Lady' (below) waits at Plymouth station to go light engine to Laira TMD on 21st July 1976 after working an express from the east.

Penzance :

With less than 8 months to go before withdrawal of the Class on BR, a rather well turned out No.D1013 'Western Ranger' (above) stands at the head of an unidentified passenger express at Penzance station on 19th July 1976, bound for at least Plymouth. In fact, No.1013 was one of the lucky ones, making it through to the last day and into preservation. She was purchased on 14th May 1977 by Mr Richard Holdsworth, under care of the Western Locomotive Association and, on 14th June 1977, she was hauled to the Torbay Steam Railway at Kingswear by (coincidentally?) Class 47 No.47013.

Penzance Shed (84D) :

It's just another dismal day with poor light, but a brace of Class 52s (above) on Penzance shed help to brighten things up on 25th May 1974 ...... No.D1068 'Western Reliance' (left) and No.D1067 'Western Druid' (right) await their next turns of duty - 1B89 and 1A79 which may, or may not, be their next outings. A third Class 52 along with a Class 47 are also on the shed.

'Western Tribute'

26th February 1977 : End of an era .... the very last day of Class 52 working and the event is suitably marked with a double-headed special excursion, the 'Western Tribute'. Running Paddington - Swansea - Bristol - Plymouth - Paddington, the train is seen headed by No.D1013 'Western Ranger' and No.D1023 'Western Fusilier' (above) and is passing Cardiff heading west to Swansea. Keen to get a viewpoint away from the masses, some ventured further west from Cardiff General for a shot.

A very busy scene to mark the occasion at Bristol, Nos.D1013 and No.D1023 (below) take the centre road through Bristol Temple Meads heading west on the next leg of their journey. The blue exhaust seen on the right is from No.D1010 'Western Campaigner' and No.D1048 'Western Lady', which are out of shot on Bath Road TMD as back up - in fact, these two followed the train down to Plymouth shortly afterwards.

Acknowledgements

My sincere thanks go to all the contributors named below who have kindly supplied images for inclusion in this edition of 'LOCO REVIEW', without which this book would not be possible. I have also included a note of any respective website addresses.

Craig Adamson (flickr.com/photos/37260)
Richard Armstrong (richard-armstrong.smugmug.com)
Alastair Blackwood (flickr.com/photos/alastairblackwood)
Ross Byers (flickr.com/photos/47222)
Edward Clarkson
Ian Cuthbertson (flickr.com/photos/locohunter)
Michael Davies (flickr.com/photos/32755955@N05)
Nigel Gibbs (flickr.com/photos/gibbo53)
Michael Groom
Neil Harvey flickr.com/neil_harvey_railway_photos)
Alan Hazelden (alanhazelden.smugmug.com)
Derek Holmes
Simon Howard (sisuktrainpix.smugmug.com)
Richard A Jones (flickr.com/photos/richardajones)
Steven King (stevekingrailphotos.weebly.com)
Keith McGovern (flickr.com/photos/16359167@N07)
Alan Padley (flickr.com/photos/alanpadley)
Dave Purser (davepurser.smugmug.com)
Robert Sherwood (southwestrailways.webs.com)
Nathan Seddon
Nick Slocombe (nick86235.smugmug.com)
David Stracey
Mick Tindall
Mark Walker (flickr.com/photos/mark-walker)
James Welham (flickr.com/photos/jameswelham)
Syd Young (flickr.com/photos/sydpix)

Eliot Andersen (cumbria.smugmug.com)
Ian Ball (northeastheavy60.uk)
Steven Brykajlo (steve-b24.smugmug.com)
Stuart Chapman
Martin Cook (flickr.com/photos/martin_cook1044)
Stephen Dance (flickr.com/photos/d1059)
Colin Dixon (flickr.com/photos/farmer55)
Carl Gorse (flickr.com/photos/37682)
David Hamilton
David Hayes (flickr.com/photos/davidhayes)
Mike Hemming (flickr.com/photos/d1021)
Guy Houston (flickr.com/photos/37001)
John Hurst
Fred Kerr
Lee Marshall (leemarshall.smugmug.com)
Robin Morel
Chris Perkins (transportmedia.smugmug.com)
Jim Ramsay (tayrail.smugmug.com)
James Skoyles (catcliffedemon.smugmug.com)
Peter Slater (railshotsuk.com)
Jamie Squibbs (jamiesquibbs.com)
Mark Thomas (markthomas-railpics.co.uk)
John Tomlin
David Weake (dwrailwayphotos.weebly.com)
Michael Wright (mawrailphotography.zenfolio.com)

(above) : Heading off to pastures new .... following overhaul by Europhoenix, two Class 87 locos are made available for lease in the UK or Europe. The locos have been finished to European standards but, unlike the '87s' exported to Bulgaria, their UK-specific equipment has been retained for use in the UK. On 28th August, WCRC Class 47 No.47500 tows No.87023 'Velocity' and No.87017 'Iron Duke' through Milton Malsor, Northamptonshire, running as 0Z87, the 12:59 Long Marston - Willesden. **Nigel Gibbs**